FRACTURED LANDS

Scott Anderson is a veteran war correspondent who has reported from Lebanon, Israel, Egypt, Northern Ireland, Chechnya, Sudan, Bosnia, El Salvador, and many other strife-torn countries. He is a contributing writer for *The New York Times Magazine*, and his work has also appeared in *Vanity Fair*, *Esquire*, *Harper's*, and *Outside*. He is the author of the novels *Moonlight Hotel* and *Triage* and the nonfiction books *Lawrence in Arabia*, *The Man Who Tried to Save the World*, and *The 4 O'Clock Murders*, as well as the coauthor of *War Zones* and *Inside the League* with his brother, Jon Lee Anderson.

ALSO BY SCOTT ANDERSON

NONFICTION

Lawrence in Arabia

The 4 O'Clock Murders

The Man Who Tried to Save the World

WITH JON LEE ANDERSON

Inside the League

War Zones

FICTION

Triage

Moonlight Hotel

FRACTURED LANDS

How the Arab World Came Apart

SCOTT ANDERSON

PICADOR

First published 2017 by Anchor Books,
a division of Penguin Random House LLC, New York

First published in the UK in paperback 2017 by Picador
an imprint of Pan Macmillan
20 New Wharf Road, London N1 9RR
Associated companies throughout the world
www.panmacmillan.com

ISBN 978-1-5098-5296-3

Copyright © Scott Anderson, 2016, 2017

The right of Scott Anderson to be identified as the
author of this work has been asserted by him in accordance
with the Copyright, Designs and Patents Act 1988.

This is an expanded version of the text that originally appeared in *The New York Times Magazine*
on August 14, 2016. All photographs © Paolo Pellegrin/Magnum Photos.

All rights reserved. No part of this publication may be reproduced,
stored in a retrieval system, or transmitted, in any form, or by any means
(electronic, mechanical, photocopying, recording or otherwise)
without the prior written permission of the publisher.

Pan Macmillan does not have any control over, or any responsibility for,
any author or third-party websites referred to in or on this book.

1 3 5 7 9 8 6 4 2

A CIP catalogue record for this book is available from the British Library.

Printed and bound by CPI Group (UK) Ltd, Croydon, CR0 4YY

This book is sold subject to the condition that it shall not, by way of
trade or otherwise, be lent, hired out, or otherwise circulated without
the publisher's prior consent in any form of binding or cover other than
that in which it is published and without a similar condition including
this condition being imposed on the subsequent purchaser.

Visit **www.picador.com** to read more about all our books
and to buy them. You will also find features, author interviews and
news of any author events, and you can sign up for e-newsletters
so that you're always first to hear about our new releases.

For Natasha, with unending love and gratitude

PREFACE

FOR OUR DRIVE into northern Iraq, Dr. Azar Mirkhan changed from his Western clothes into the traditional dress of a Kurdish Peshmerga warrior: a tight-fitting, short woolen jacket over his shirt, baggy pantaloons, and a wide cummerbund. He also thought to bring along certain accessories. These included a combat knife that tucked neatly into the waist of his cummerbund, a loaded .45 automatic, and sniper binoculars. Should matters turn particularly ticklish, his M4 assault rifle lay within easy reach on the backseat, with extra magazines in the footwell. The doctor shrugged. "It's a bad neighborhood."

Our destination that day in May 2015 was the place of Azar's greatest sorrow, one that haunted him still. The previous year, ISIS gunmen had cut a murderous swath through northern Iraq, brushing away an Iraqi army vastly greater in size, and then turned their attention to the Kurds. Azar had divined precisely where the ISIS killers were about to strike next, knew that tens of thousands of civilians stood helpless in their path, but had been unable to get anyone to heed his warnings. In desperation, he had loaded up his car with guns and raced to the scene, only to come to a spot in the road where he saw he was just hours too late. "It was obvious," Azar said, "so obvious. But no one wanted to listen." On that day, we were returning to the place where the fabled Kurdish warriors of northern Iraq had been out-maneuvered and put to flight, where Dr. Azar Mirkhan had failed to avert a colossal tragedy—and where, for many more months to come, he would continue to battle ISIS.

Azar is a practicing urologist, but even without the fire-power and warrior getup, the forty-one-year-old would exude the aura of a hunter. He walks with a curious loping gait that produces little sound, and in conversation has a tendency to tuck in his chin and stare from beneath heavy-lidded eyes, rather as if he were sighting down a gun. With his prominent nose and jet-black pompadour, he bears a passing resemblance to a young Johnny Cash.

The weaponry also complemented the doctor's personal philosophy, as expressed in a scene from one of his favorite movies, *The Good, the Bad, and the Ugly*, when a bathing Eli Wallach is caught off guard by a man seeking to kill him. Rather than immediately shoot Wallach, the would-be assassin goes into a triumphant soliloquy, allowing Wal-lach to kill him first.

"'When you have to shoot, shoot; don't talk,'" Azar quoted from the movie. "That is us Kurds now. This is not the time to talk, but to shoot."

Azar is one of six people whose lives are chronicled in these pages. The six are from different regions, different cities, different tribes, different families, but they share, along with millions of other people in and from the Middle East, an experience of profound unraveling. Their lives have been forever altered by upheavals that began in 2003 with the American invasion of Iraq, and then accelerated with the series of revolutions and insurrections that have collectively become known in the West as the Arab Spring. They continue today with the depredations of ISIS, with terrorist attacks, and with failing states.

For each of these six people, the upheavals were crystallized by a specific, singular event. For Azar Mirkhan, it came on the road to Sinjar, when he saw that his worst fears had come true. For Laila Soueif in Egypt, it came when a young man separated from a sprinting mass of protesters to embrace her, and she thought she knew the revolution would succeed. For Majdi el-Mangoush in Libya, it came as he walked across a deadly no-man's-land and, overwhelmed by a sudden euphoria, felt free for the first time in his life. For Khulood al-Zaidi in Iraq, it came when, with just a few menacing words from a former friend, she finally understood that everything she had worked for was gone. For Majd Ibrahim in Syria, it came when, watching an interrogator search his cell phone for the identity of his "controller," he knew his own execution was drawing nearer by the moment. For Wakaz Hassan in Iraq, a young man with no apparent interest in politics or religion, it came on the day ISIS gunmen showed up in his village and offered him a choice.

As disparate as these moments were, for each of these six people they represented a crossing-over, passage to a place from which there will never be a return. Such changes, of course—multiplied by millions of lives—are also transforming their homelands, the greater Middle East, and, by inevitable extension, the entire world.

But for all the abruptness with which these changes occurred, they didn't come completely without warning. History is always a result of seemingly random currents and incidents, the significance of which can be determined—or, more often, disputed—only in hindsight. In trying to parse out what has happened in the Middle East, one can point to some clues that are very recent, others that are centuries old.

WHILE ABSENTLY FIDDLING with his homemade fly whisk—several sprigs of dried rosemary held together with a piece of aluminum foil—the sixty-year-old man in the brown-tinted sunglasses gazed meditatively up at the shadowing palm fronds.

"The history of mankind is not fixed," he muttered after a time, "and it does not go at one pace. Sometimes it moves at a steady pace, and sometimes it is very fast. It is very flexible all the time." He set the fly whisk on the cheap plastic patio table and turned in my direction. "The past stage was the era of nationalism—of the identity of one nation—and now, suddenly, that has changed. It is the era of globalization, and there are many new factors which are mapping out the world."

On the topic of changing times, the man in the sunglasses could speak with a certain authority. He was Muammar el-Qaddafi, the dictator of Libya, and by the time I met with him in October 2002, he had successfully navigated the shifting geopolitical shoals of the region to remain in power for thirty-three years. That agility also helped explain my presence at the Bab al-Azizia barracks in Tripoli. By late 2002, the drumbeat for war against Saddam Hussein in Iraq was reaching a crescendo in Washington, and there was talk in President Bush's inner circle that, once the Iraqi despot was dispensed with, the troublesome Libyan would be next. To forestall that, Qaddafi had recently taken a number of steps to bring himself in from the cold, and these included a fledgling public relations push. That autumn, the famously reclusive dictator granted some of his first foreign media interviews in over a decade.

But if by his actions Qaddafi exhibited some nervousness about his relations with the Bush administration, he displayed none at all when it came to his standing with the Libyan people. After over three decades in power, he had become such an omnipresent figure in the lives of his countrymen that they rarely even referred to him by name anymore. He was simply "the Leader." One measure of his confidence showed when, after I asked how he wished to be remembered, he chose to have some fun with the answer, turning it into a joke both self-aware and cynical. "I would hope that people would feel that I haven't been selfish," he began, "that I have even forsaken myself in order to please and to help others. I do hope people would say that." He leaned close and gave a low chuckle. "And I do hope that I have actually been like this in reality."

The irony, of course, is that the Americans didn't come for Qaddafi—at least not then. Instead, the Leader would remain on his perch in Tripoli for another decade, only to be done in by a danger he didn't foresee: a revolt by his own people. In the series of popular insurrections and revolutions that began sweeping the Middle East in the first days of 2011, Muammar el-Qaddafi was destined to be one of its most famous—and most gruesomely dispatched—victims, murdered by a lynch mob on the shoulder of a Libyan highway.

THE EVENT CREDITED with setting off the Arab Spring could hardly have been more improbable: the suicide by immolation of a poor Tunisian fruit-and-vegetable seller in protest over government harassment. By the time Mohamed Bouazizi succumbed to his injuries on January 4, 2011, the protesters who initially took to Tunisia's streets calling for economic reform were demanding the resignation of the nation's strongman president of twenty-three years, Zine el-Abidine Ben Ali. In subsequent days, those demonstrations grew in size and intensity—and then they jumped Tunisia's border. By the end of January, antigovernment protests had erupted in Algeria, Egypt, Oman, and Jordan. That was only the beginning. By November, just ten months after Bouazizi's death, four long-standing Middle Eastern dictatorships had been toppled, a half dozen other suddenly embattled regimes had undergone shake-ups or had promised reforms, and antigovernment demonstrations—some peaceful, others violent—had spread in an arc across the Arab world from Mauritania to Bahrain.

By the time of the Arab Spring revolts, my familiarity

with the Middle East dated back nearly forty years. As a young boy in the early 1970s, I had traveled through the region with my father, a journey that sparked both my fascination with Islam and my love of the desert. The Middle East was also the site of my first foray into journalism when, in the summer of 1983, I hopped on a plane to the embattled city of Beirut in hopes of finding work as a stringer. In journalistic pursuits over the subsequent years, I had embedded with Israeli commandos conducting raids in the West Bank; dined with Janjaweed raiders in Darfur; interviewed the families of suicide bombers. Ultimately, I took a five-year hiatus from magazine journalism to write a book on the historical origins of the modern Middle East.

From these experiences, I initially welcomed the convulsions of the Arab Spring—indeed, I believed they were long overdue. In my professional travels over the decades, I had found no other corner of the globe to rival the Arab world in its utter stagnation. While Qaddafi set a record for longevity in the area with his forty-two-year dictatorship, it was not that different elsewhere; by 2011, any Egyptian younger than forty-one—and that was roughly 75 percent of the population—had only ever known two heads of state, while a Syrian of the same age had lived his or her entire life under the control of the father-and-son al-Assad dynasty. Along with political stasis, in many Arab nations most levers of economic power lay in the hands of small oligarchies or aristocratic families; for everyone else, about the only path to financial security was to wrangle a job within fantastically bloated public-sector bureaucracies, government agencies that were often themselves monuments to nepotism and corruption. While the sheer amount of money pouring into oil-rich, sparsely populated nations like Libya or Kuwait might allow for a degree of economic trickle-down prosperity, this was not at all the case in more populous but resource-poor nations like Egypt or Syria, where poverty and underemployment were severe and—given the ongoing regional population explosion—ever-worsening problems.

What I also found heartening in the Arab Spring's early days was the focus of the people's wrath. One of the Arab world's most prominent and debilitating features, I had long felt, was a culture of grievance. These societies seemed to me to be defined less by what people aspired to than by what they opposed. They were anti-Zionist, anti-West, anti-imperialist. For generations, the region's dictators had been adroit at channeling public frustration toward these external "enemies" and away from their own misrule. But with the Arab Spring, that old playbook suddenly didn't work anymore. Instead, and for the first time on such a mass scale, the people of the Middle East were directing their rage squarely at the regimes themselves.

Then it all went horribly wrong. By the summer of 2012, two of the "freed" nations—Libya and Yemen—were sliding into anarchy and factionalism, while the struggle against the Bashar al-Assad regime in Syria had descended into vicious civil war. In Egypt the following summer, the nation's first democratically elected government was overthrown by the military, a coup cheered on by many of the same young activists who had taken to the streets to demand democracy two years earlier. The only truly bright spot among the Arab Spring nations was the place where it started, Tunisia, but even there, terrorist attacks and feuding politicians were a constant threat to a fragile government. Amid the chaos, the remnants of Osama bin Laden's old outfit, Al Qaeda, gained a new lease on life, resurrected the war in Iraq, and then spawned an even more murderous offshoot: Islamic State, or ISIS.

WHY DID IT turn out this way? Why did a movement begun with such high promise go so terribly awry?

The difficulty in coming up with a single answer is the very scattershot nature of the Arab Spring, the lack of apparent pattern between those nations radically transformed by its upheavals and others, often right next door, that were barely touched. Some of the nations in crisis were wealthy by regional standards (Libya), others crushingly poor (Yemen). Some countries with comparatively benign dictatorships (Tunisia) blew up along with some of the area's most brutal (Syria). The same wide range of political and economic disparity is seen in the nations that remained stable.

If not a complete answer, at least a clue came to me when I recalled a conversation I had with a Jordanian man in the early days of the turmoil.

I had hired Hassan as my driver for an extended tour of Jordan, and over the course of five days together we became friends. Gregarious and well educated, he prided himself on his modernity and took every opportunity to denounce the rise of Islamic fundamentalism in the region. One striking facet of Hassan's personality was an abiding adoration of Jordan's king, Abdullah II, his face lighting up at the mere mention of his name. But even this was tied to Hassan's modernist outlook. "He is very progressive and has done many things to enlighten the people," he would say of Abdullah. "Because of him, Jordan is now the most Western of all Arab nations."

In view of such pronouncements, I was caught a bit off guard by Hassan's comments when, one evening, we fell to discussing the role of tribalism in the region and the braking effect it often exerted on the liberal ideas he embraced. After agreeing this was an enormous problem, Hassan took a deep pull on his cigarette. "I am not at all proud to say this," he said, "but if ever I were forced to choose between the king and my family"—by which he meant his tribe— "then of course I would choose my family. In fact, it isn't even a matter of choice. Whatever the reason, if my family went against the state, then so would I."

It was a statement I might have expected in Yemen or rural Sudan, but not from this "modern man" in one of the Middle East's most cosmopolitan nations. But it was a reminder that in much of the Arab world, the ancient pull of one's tribe, of one's blood, still remains just beneath the surface of things. It also offered a starting point, an organizing principle of sorts, with which to consider the Arab Spring.

While most of the twenty-two nations that make up the Arab world have been buffeted to some degree by the Arab Spring, of the six most profoundly affected—Egypt, Iraq, Libya, Syria, Tunisia, and Yemen—none are monarchies.

All are republics. Might this reveal inherent fault lines in the structure of Arab republics? Put another way, as corrupt and repressive as many of the Arab monarchies are, could it be that they withstood the pressures of the Arab Spring because of a kind of internal tribal compact that some of their republican neighbors lacked?

These questions become especially salient with regard to the three Arab republics that have disintegrated so completely as to raise doubt that they will ever again exist as functioning states: Iraq, Syria, and Libya. Although separated by geography, history, economics, and any number of other factors, what all three share is membership in that small list of Arab countries artificially created by Western imperial powers in the early twentieth century. In each, little thought was given to national coherence, and even less to tribal or sectarian divisions. Certainly, these same internal divisions exist in many of the region's other republics, as well as in its monarchies, but it would seem undeniable that those two elements operating in concert—the lack of an intrinsic sense of national identity, joined to a form of government that supplanted the traditional organizing principle of society—left Iraq, Syria, and Libya especially vulnerable when the storms of change descended.

From this, it would appear that Muammar el-Qaddafi had it precisely backward when he opined that the age of nationalism was giving way to a new age of globalization. Instead, in "artificial" Arab countries like his own, the Arab Spring meant a reversion to the most basic of social orders, in which ancient loyalties would sweep away not only him but also the very nationalism he had tried to instill. In fact, all but one of the six people profiled in this book are from these artificial states, and their individual stories are rooted in the larger story of how those nations came to be.

In the context of this history, the 2011 suicide of Mohamed Bouazizi seems less the catalyst for the Arab Spring than a culmination of tensions and contradictions that had been simmering under the surface of Arab society for a long time. Indeed, throughout the Arab world, residents are far more likely to point to a different event, one that occurred eight years before Bouazizi's death, as the moment when the process of disintegration began: the American invasion of Iraq. Many even point to a singular image that embodied that upheaval. It came on the afternoon of April 9, 2003, in the Firdos Square of downtown Baghdad, when, with the help of a winch and an American M88 armored recovery vehicle, a towering statue of Iraqi dictator, Saddam Hussein, was pulled to the ground.

While today that image is remembered in the Arab world with resentment—the symbolism of this latest Western intervention in their region was quite inescapable— at the time it spurred something far more nuanced. For the first time in their lives, what Syrians and Libyans and other Arabs just as much as Iraqis saw was that a figure as seemingly immovable as Saddam Hussein could be cast aside, that the political and social paralysis that had gripped their collective lands for so long might actually be broken. Not nearly so apparent was that these strongmen had actually exerted considerable energy to bind up their nations, and in their absence the ancient forces of tribalism and sectarianism would begin to exert their own centrifugal pull.

Colonel Muammar el-Qaddafi in Tripoli, October 2002

Even less apparent was how these forces would both attract and repel the United States, tarnishing its power and prestige in the region to an extent from which it might never recover.

But at least one man saw this quite clearly. For much of 2002, the Bush administration had laid the groundwork for the Iraq invasion by accusing Saddam Hussein of pursuing a weapons-of-mass-destruction program and obliquely linking him to the September 11 attacks of Osama bin Laden. In my interview with Muammar el-Qaddafi that October, six months before Firdos Square, I had asked him who would benefit if the Iraq invasion actually occurred. The Libyan dictator had a habit of theatrically pondering before answering my questions, but his reply to that one was instantaneous. "Bin Laden," he said. "There is no doubt about that. And Iraq could end up becoming the staging ground for Al Qaeda, because if the Saddam government collapses, it will be anarchy in Iraq. If that happens, actions against Americans will be considered jihad."

THIS BOOK IS in the form of six individual narratives, which, woven within the larger strands of history, aim to provide a tapestry of an Arab world in revolt. The account is divided into five parts, which proceed chronologically. Along with introducing several of these individuals, part 1 focuses on three historical factors that are crucial to understanding the current crisis: the inherent instability of the Middle East's artificial states; the precarious position in which U.S.-allied Arab governments have found themselves when compelled to pursue policies bitterly opposed by their own people; and American involvement in the de facto partitioning of Iraq twenty-five years ago, an event little remarked upon at the time—and barely more so since—that helped call into question the very legitimacy of the modern Arab nation-state. Part 2 is primarily devoted to the American invasion of Iraq and to how it laid the groundwork for the Arab Spring revolts. Part 3 follows the explosive outcome of those revolts as they occurred in Egypt, Libya, and Syria. By part 4, which chronicles the rise of ISIS, and part 5, which tracks the resulting exodus from the region, we are squarely in the present, at the heart of the world's gravest concern.

I have tried to tell a human story, one that has its share of heroes, even some glimmers of hope. But what follows, ultimately, is a dark warning. Today the tragedy and violence of the Middle East have spilled from its banks, with nearly a million Syrians and Iraqis flooding into Europe to escape the wars in their homelands, and terrorist attacks in Dhaka, Paris, and beyond. With the ISIS cause being invoked by mass murderers in San Bernardino and Orlando and Munich, the issues of immigration and terrorism have become conjoined in many Westerners' minds, and proved a key political flash point in both the June 2016 Brexit vote in Great Britain and the 2016 American presidential election. In some sense, it is fitting that the turmoil in the Arab world has its roots in the First World War, for like that war, it is a regional crisis that has come quickly and widely—with little seeming reason or logic—to influence events at every corner of the globe.

PART I

Origins

1972–2003

INTRODUCTION

AS FANCIFUL AS it might seem today, there was a time when the Arab world was not only acquiescent to American involvement in its affairs but fairly clamored for it. This occurred at an absolutely crucial moment in the political evolution of the Middle East, the summer of 1919, and began when a small group of American officials set sail from France for Syria with a lofty goal. While its efforts have been largely airbrushed from history, the King-Crane Commission had the opportunity to fundamentally alter the Middle Eastern chessboard we know today.

For most of the previous four hundred years, the Arab lands of the Middle East had been under the rule of the Ottoman Empire. Quite aware of their technological and military backwardness in comparison to their European imperial rivals, the Ottoman sultans had cleverly converted weakness into a virtue by ruling with a very light touch; so long as the locals in their far-flung empire paid their taxes and met military conscription quotas, they were pretty much left to themselves. Most remarkable was how this laissez-faire approach extended to political organization. In recognition of the Arab world's fantastically complex social order of tribes and subtribes and clans, joined to the region's myriad religious groupings, the Ottomans divided their empire into a patchwork of largely autonomous provinces, or *vilayets*. Further, under the *milliyet* ("nationalities") system, each minority religious community was effectively self-governing, overseen by its own religious courts that superseded Ottoman law. These progressive arrangements stood in sharp contrast to the conversion-by-the-sword tactics employed by most European powers at the time.

But in 1914, the Ottomans made a fatal mistake. By joining with Germany and Austro-Hungary on the losing side of World War I, the Ottomans left themselves defenseless against the designs of the victorious imperial powers, Great Britain and France. Having previously seized the Ottomans' North African territories—most notably, Egypt and Algeria—the British and French at the 1919 Paris Peace Conference set their sights on the Arab heartland itself. Under the terms of the once-secret Sykes-Picot Agreement, that heartland was to be carved up into spheres of British and French control. Any expectation that the Europeans might administer these lands with Ottoman-style finesse was belied by the nickname that officials in the British Foreign Office gave their enterprise: "the Great Loot."

But there stood one potential obstacle in the European imperialists' path: U.S. president Woodrow Wilson. Having brought the United States into World War I on the promise of ending the age of imperialism, at Paris he eloquently argued for the self-determination of "small states." When this high-minded sentiment met with the stiff resistance of his British and French allies, Wilson did what politicians are wont to do in such circumstances: he formed a committee. It was this committee, the King-Crane Commission, that sailed into Jaffa Port on the morning of June 10, 1919. On a mission quite without precedent for the time, they had come to poll the local inhabitants on just what sort of governance they desired.

For nearly two months, the commission traveled through Turkey and greater Syria, holding town hall–style meetings with delegations from most every conceivable ethnic and religious bloc. From these gatherings emerged a startlingly uniform consensus. No one wanted to be ruled by the British, and even less by the French. Rather, they wanted independence or, barring that, an American administration, or mandate.

The King-Crane delegation dutifully wrote up their explosive findings during the return journey to France, with the unanimous recommendation that the United States assume the mandate for Syria. In this proposal, however, they had seriously misread the American president. While eager to lecture his European allies on their moral obligations, Woodrow Wilson was loath that the United States itself should assume foreign responsibilities. With the commission's inconvenient findings now only a potential embarrassment, its reports were simply locked away in a safe, not to be seen or read by anyone until they were leaked by *The New York Times* three years later. By then, "the Great Loot" had transpired, and with it the creation of

those artificial borders that would be torn apart so extravagantly nearly one hundred years later in the Arab Spring.
Also established was a precedent for American inconstancy,
a habit of raising hopes in the Arab world and then dashing
them in a pattern that would be repeated many times over
the next century.

In Mesopotamia, the British joined together three Ottoman *vilayets* and named it Iraq. The southernmost of these
provinces was dominated by Shiite Arabs, the central by
Sunni Arabs, and the northernmost by non-Arab Kurds.
To the west of Iraq, the European powers took the opposite approach, carving the vast lands of "greater Syria" into
smaller, more manageable parcels. Falling under French
rule was the smaller rump state of Syria—essentially the
nation that exists today—and the coastal enclave of Lebanon, while the British took Palestine and Transjordan,
a swath of southern Syria that would eventually become
Israel and Jordan. Coming a bit later to the game, in 1934,
Italy joined the three ancient North African regions that it
had wrested from the Ottomans in 1912 to form the colony
of Libya.

To maintain dominion over these fractious territories,
the European powers adopted the same divide-and-conquer
approach that had served them so well in the colonization
of sub-Saharan Africa in the late nineteenth century. This
consisted of empowering a local ethnic or religious minority to serve as their local administrators, confident that this
minority would never rebel against their foreign overseers
lest they be engulfed by the disenfranchised majority.

To this end, in Iraq the British brought over one of their Arabian wartime allies, Faisal Hussein, and installed him as king—never mind that Faisal had absolutely no ties to the region. His monarchy established Sunni primacy in a Shiite-majority state. The French did the opposite in Sunni-majority Syria, empowering the Alawites, a Shiite splinter sect, along with the Christian minority to serve as their local intermediaries. In Libya, the Italians came up with a novel approach: given the deep-seated rivalry that existed between its principal regions, Tripolitania and Cyrenaica, the Italians made each region's largest city, Tripoli and Benghazi, respectively, a co-capital of the new nation.

This was only the most overt level of the Europeans' divide-and-conquer strategy. Beneath the sectarian and regional divisions in these "nations" there lay the intricate tapestry of tribe and subtribe and clan, ancient social orders that remained the populations' principal source of identification and allegiance. Much as the United States Army and white settlers did with Indian tribes in the conquest of the American West, so the British and French and Italians proved adept at pitting these groups against one another, bestowing favors—weapons or food or sinecures—to one faction in return for fighting another. The great difference is that in the American West, the settlers stayed and the tribal system was essentially destroyed. In the Arab world, the Europeans would eventually leave, but the sectarian and tribal schisms they fueled remained.

Through the first half of the twentieth century, these arrangements proved quite durable. Much of this had to do with the enduring poverty and limited technological state of the region. By playing to the benefit of the small local elite, and by upholding the authority of their local pliant ruler, the European imperial powers and their allied corporate interests could rather ignore whatever resentments were building beneath the surface. On those occasions when the resentments did bubble to the surface, swift and brutal action was taken. The most extreme example of this was the Senussi rebellion against Italian rule in Libya's Cyrenaica province in the late 1920s. By the time the rebellion was crushed in 1930, an estimated one-quarter of Cyrenaica's population had been killed through Italian poison gas attacks and mass executions. In British-ruled Egypt and Iraq, dominance was retained by more subtle means. While granting both nations nominal independence, Egypt in 1922 and Iraq in 1932, the British inserted "mutual assistance" clauses in the independence charters that enshrined both a continued British military presence and control over their foreign affairs.

It all began to change—and rapidly—at the end of World War II. With the British and French empires clearly in a state of terminal decline, nationalist groups throughout the Middle East, as elsewhere in the developing world, began clamoring for independence. At the same time, vast new oil finds in Saudi Arabia and Iraq were converting the region from an economic backwater into a place of vital geopolitical importance. Further awakening political consciousness was the 1948 creation of the state of Israel, a development that caused outrage throughout the Arab world. By the early 1950s, all that was needed to bring Arab nationalism to full flower, it seemed, was the emergence of a charismatic leader who might speak to both the aspirations and frustrations of the Arab people. That leader was found in the form of a thirty-four-year-old Egyptian lieutenant colonel named Gamal Abdel Nasser.

1

Laila Soueif
Egypt

AT THE GARDEN café in Cairo, Laila Soueif stubbed out the remnants of her dying cigarette, gave a short cough, then lit another.

For the past thirty-four years, Laila, sixty-one, has been a professor of mathematics at Cairo University, but she is best known to the Egyptian public for her ubiquity at antigovernment street demonstrations. If her radical politics have mellowed somewhat over the years, she remains instantly recognizable at these rallies by her hair. In a culture where women of a certain age and class invariably style and dye their hair black, hers is a short and unruly mop of gray.

The youngest daughter of college professors, Laila was born into a life of both privilege and intellectual freedom (her older sister, Ahdaf Soueif, is one of Egypt's best-known contemporary novelists), and gravitated toward social activism at an early age. This was actually encouraged under Nasser's rule, albeit within limits.

"The state was repressive in the Nasserist era," she said, "but at the same time, you could accomplish a lot of good

Laila Soueif at her home in Cairo

away from politics. If you concentrated your energies there, in building up civic institutions—and that is what my parents did—you would be left alone."

Laila attended her first overtly political rally when she was just sixteen. It was 1972, two years after Nasser's death, and the protesters were demanding what students have so often desired—a more equitable world, greater freedom of expression. But they also had a demand more specific to the Arab world: that Nasser's successor, Anwar Sadat, launch a war to recover the Sinai Peninsula, which had been seized by Israel in the Six-Day War of 1967. From this experience, Laila would soon be convinced of the power of civil disobedience; Sadat did, in fact, launch an attack on Israel the following year. What Laila hadn't counted on was the more immediate wrath of her parents. Just two hours after she joined the protest in Cairo's Tahrir Square, Laila's mother and father tracked down their teenage daughter and dragged her home. "From that, I learned that it was easier to defy the state than to defy my parents," she said.

But that experience also set Laila Soueif on a path from which she wouldn't waver. While studying mathematics at Cairo University in the mid-1970s, she met her future husband, Ahmed Seif, who was already the leader of an underground communist student cell calling for revolution. By then, Egypt had long been regarded as the political capital of the Middle East, the birthplace of revolutionary movements and ideas, and it had cemented that reputation in the modern era through Nasser's leadership.

Quickly emerging as the most dynamic personality of the Free Officers Movement, the cabal of junior military officers who overthrew Egypt's Western-pliant king in 1952, Nasser championed the causes of "Arab socialism" and pan-Arab unity. Almost as swiftly, he became a galvanizing figure throughout the Arab world, the spokesman for a people long dominated by foreigners and Western-educated elites. Just as crucial to the strongman's popularity was what he opposed: colonialism, imperialism, and that most immediate and enduring example of the West's meddling in the region, the state of Israel.

But Nasser's fiery pronouncements notwithstanding, at least initially, his rise seemed to offer the United States a renewed opportunity for good standing in the Arab world. Much like Woodrow Wilson in World War I, President Franklin Delano Roosevelt had envisioned the aftermath of World War II as the end of the colonial age and the advent of a new and cooperative world order, his cherished United

Nations taking its inspiration from Wilson's failed League of Nations. Roosevelt's dream had been quickly supplanted by the Cold War between the United States and the Soviet Union, with his successors—first Harry S. Truman and then Dwight D. Eisenhower—showing far less interest in spreading democracy or dismantling the prewar order than in shoring up anti-Soviet proxy states. For a time, Nasser presented something of a wild card in this equation, and the United States sought to woo the young Egyptian leader to its side through a combination of extravagant promises and veiled threats. When that effort spectacularly foundered—the final straw came when the Eisenhower administration blocked Western funding for Nasser's Aswan Dam project, hastening the Soviet Union's arrival with checkbook in hand—it helped burnish Nasser's anti-West credentials. His status in the Arab world soared to meteoric new heights when he faced down Britain, France, and Israel in the 1956 Suez Crisis.

Nasser's success inspired many other would-be Arab leaders, and nowhere more so than in the artificial states of the Middle East left behind by the European powers. By 1968, military officers espousing the Baathist ("renaissance") philosophy—a quasi-socialist form of Pan-Arabism—had seized power in Iraq and Syria. They were joined the following year by the Libyan lieutenant Muammar el-Qaddafi and his somewhat baffling "third universal theory," which rejected traditional democracy in favor of rule by "people's committees." In all three countries, just as in Egypt, Western-favored monarchs or parliaments were neutered or cast aside. And just as in Egypt, in all three, the dictators tilted toward alliance with the Soviets, and rallied their countrymen with calls for the destruction of Israel.

But Nasser possessed an advantage that his fellow autocrats in the region did not. With a sense of national identity that stretched back millennia, Egypt never seemed in serious danger of being torn apart; the centrifugal pull of tribes or clans or sectarian identity didn't exist there to anywhere near the degree it did in Syria or Iraq. And while Egypt's ideological spectrum ran from secular communists to fundamentalist Islamists, Nasser could forge a national consensus across this fractious political landscape by appealing both to Egyptian national pride and to a shared antipathy for the West, a vestige, perhaps, of seventy years of heavy-handed rule by Britain.

Thus, even when Islamist conservatives became alarmed by Nasser's moves toward greater secularism, most still saw him as a hero for nationalizing Western businesses, for his implacable opposition to Israel, and for emerging victorious in the Suez Crisis. Similarly, urban liberals like the Soueif family, who disdained Nasser's strong-arm rule—his was a military dictatorship, after all—also cheered him for his leadership in the international Nonaligned Movement, for proudly thumbing his nose at the United States as it sought to compel Egypt into its Cold War orbit. This, then, became the means by which Nasser, and his successor, Anwar Sadat, maintained their grip on power: play left and right off against each other as a matter of course; bring them together when needed by focusing on an external foe. Such maneuvering resulted in many odd political turns, including that first pro-war protest march of Laila Soueif.

After working on leftist causes together throughout their time at Cairo University, Laila and Ahmed married in 1978. That same year, Egypt's political landscape was neatly turned upside down when Sadat signed the Camp David Accords, leading to an American-brokered peace treaty with Israel. This stunning about-face was the culmination of Sadat's gradual retreat from Nasser's pan-Arab ideals—and from Egypt's long flirtation with the Soviet Union—but it also simultaneously propelled Egypt into the camp of American client states and isolated her from much of the rest of the Arab world. Even more ominously for Sadat, what was seen in the West as an act of courage was regarded by many Egyptians as an act of betrayal and national shame. This was certainly the view of Laila and Ahmed. It was in the wake of the 1979 peace treaty that some of the men in Ahmed's underground cell began buying up arms on the black market and vowing "armed action" against the government. While those plans never got off the ground, Sadat's enemies were now to be found at all points on the political spectrum. It was a group of Islamist military plotters who finally got to the Egyptian president, assassinating Sadat at a military parade in Cairo in October 1981.

A month later, Laila gave birth to her and Ahmed's first child, a boy they named Alaa. Their lives took on an air of increasingly apolitical domesticity, and by 1983, Laila, then twenty-seven, was juggling the demands of child-rearing with her new position as a professor of mathematics at Cairo University. All normalcy was shattered, however, when Sadat's successor, Hosni Mubarak, ordered a sweeping security crackdown. Among those ensnared in the dragnet were Ahmed and his colleagues in the underground cell. Severely tortured until he signed a full confession, Ahmed was then released to await his verdict. When that verdict was returned, in late 1984, the news was grim: Ahmed was found guilty of illegal weapons possession and sentenced to five years in prison.

At the time, Laila was in France, having accepted a scholarship to further her math studies, but when Ahmed's sentence was handed down, she rushed back to Cairo with Alaa. Thanks to a curious loophole in Egyptian law, sentences for security-related offenses like Ahmed's had to be approved by the president, a process that normally took several months and during which the defendant could remain out on bail. It presented the couple with a tempting choice.

"We had to decide," Laila told me. "Does he submit and go into prison for five years, do we try to find some way to get him out of the country, or do we go into hiding?" She gave a nonchalant shrug. "So we went into hiding."

For several months, the couple lived as fugitives with their three-year-old son. Ultimately, though, both Ahmed and Laila realized it was a futile exercise. "He wasn't willing to leave the country," Laila said, "and he couldn't stay in hiding forever. He decided it was easier to do the five years, so he gave himself up." But not necessarily easier for Laila. She had become pregnant during her and Ahmed's brief time on the run, leaving her to tend to a second child, a girl they named Mona, as Ahmed served out his prison sentence.

It was in prison that Ahmed experienced something of

an epiphany. By continuing the entente with the United States and Israel that Sadat had begun, Mubarak naturally also inherited the taint of capitulation in the eyes of many of his countrymen. Unable to forge national cohesion by turning to the old external enemy card—after all, Egypt was now in bed with those supposed enemies—Mubarak had devised a more carefully calibrated system to play his secular leftist and Islamist rightist oppositions against each other. Ahmed, thrown into prison with both factions, saw firsthand how this strategy played out when it came to even the most basic of human rights. As he would later tell Joe Stork of Human Rights Watch, "The communists would say secretly, 'It doesn't matter if Islamists are tortured.' And the Islamists would say, 'Why not torture communists?'"

Vowing to fight for judicial reform, Ahmed devoted himself to studying law in his prison cell. Within a month of his release in 1989, he was admitted to the Egyptian bar.

This placed the ex-political prisoner and his wife at a crossroads. With Laila a tenured professor at Cairo University and Ahmed now a lawyer, the couple had the opportunity to carve out a comfortable existence for themselves among the Cairene elite. Instead, and at ultimately great personal cost, they would engage ever more deeply in Egypt's widening turmoil, trying to build bridges across the very ideological divides that had for so long been critical to the government's own survival.

2

Majdi el-Mangoush
Libya

A ONCE-PROSPEROUS PORT city roughly 120 miles east of Tripoli, the Libyan capital, Misurata was a main terminus of the old trans-Saharan trade route, the stopping point of camel caravans taking gold and slaves from sub-Saharan Africa for export across the Mediterranean. Ever since, it has been one of Libya's chief commercial hubs, its residents regarded as industrious and particularly capitalist-minded. Prominent among those inhabitants is the Mangoush clan, so much so that one of the oldest neighborhoods of the city bears the family name. And it was in that neighborhood on July 4, 1986, that Omar and Fatheya el-Mangoush, civil servants for the Misurata municipal government, welcomed the birth of the youngest of their six children, a boy they named Majdi.

By the time of Majdi's birth, Libya had been ruled by Muammar el-Qaddafi for seventeen years. Viewed in the West as something of a rakish enfant terrible when he and his fellow military plotters overthrew Libya's king in 1969—Qaddafi was then himself just twenty-seven—the

handsome former signal corps lieutenant was wildly popular among his countrymen in the years immediately following the coup. A key to that popularity was his emulation
of Gamal Abdel Nasser in neighboring Egypt. Like Nasser,
Qaddafi kindled Arab pride by nationalizing Western business interests, including parts of Libya's vital oil industry,
and standing in vehement opposition to the state of Israel.
By spreading the wealth around, he also enabled families
like the Mangoushes to live a comfortable middle-class life.

Over time, however, Qaddafi's rule increasingly bore
less resemblance to Egypt's "soft" dictatorship and more
to that of two others influenced by Nasser's model: the
Baathist regimes of Saddam Hussein in Iraq and Hafez
al-Assad in Syria. The parallels were quite striking. In all
three countries, the dictators developed elaborate personality cults—their faces adorned posters and murals and
postage stamps—and, unlike their Egyptian counterparts,
remained wholly aligned with the "anti-imperialist" bloc
of Arab nations, their stances helped along by deepening
ties with the Soviet Union. True to the Baathist credo of
"Arab socialism" and Qaddafi's third universal theory, all
three countries embarked on fabulously ambitious public
works projects, building hospitals and schools and colleges
throughout their lands and bankrolling those enterprises
with oil receipts (in the cases of Libya and Iraq) or through
the patronage of the Soviet Union (in the case of Syria). At
the same time, the states established extravagantly bloated
governmental structures, such that their ministries and
agencies quickly became the main pillars of the economy;
eventually more than half of the Libyan workforce—Majdi

el-Mangoush's parents among them—was on the government payroll, and the figures in Saddam Hussein's Iraq were similar. "Everybody was connected to the state somehow," Majdi explained. "For their housing, for their job. It was impossible to exist outside of it."

Yet, for all their revolutionary rhetoric, the dictators of Libya, Iraq, and Syria remained ever mindful that their nations were essentially artificial constructs. What this meant was that many of their subjects' primary loyalty lay not to the state but to their tribe or, more broadly, to their ethnic or religious sect. In the absence of such a national allegiance, compelling loyalty required both the carrot and the stick. In all three nations, the leaders entered into elaborate and labyrinthine alliances with various tribes and clans. Stay on the dictator's good side, and your tribe might be given control of a ministry or a lucrative business concession; fall on his bad side, and you're all out in the cold. The strongmen also carefully forged ties across ethnic and religious divides. In Iraq, even though most all senior Baathist officials were, like Saddam Hussein, of the Sunni minority, he endeavored to sprinkle just enough Shiites and Kurds through his administration to lend it an ecumenical sheen. In Hafez al-Assad's Sunni-majority Syria, rule by his Alawite minority was bolstered by maintaining a de facto alliance with the nation's Christian community, giving another significant minority a stake in the status quo.

This coalition-building had a unique geographic dimension in Libya. Aside from the historical divide that existed between its principal regions of Tripolitania and Cyrenaica, human settlement in Libya had always been clustered along the Mediterranean coast, and what had developed there over the millennia was essentially a series of semiautonomous city-states resistant to central rule. Thus, while Qaddafi didn't need to worry about religious sectarianism—virtually all Libyans are Sunni Muslims—he did need to think about drawing into his ruling circle the requisite number of Misuratans and Benghazinos to keep everyone mollified.

And if inducements and handshakes didn't work, there was always the stick. Libya, Iraq, and Syria erected some of the most brutal and ubiquitous state security apparatuses to be found anywhere in the world. Operating with utter impunity, the local security forces, or mukhabarat, of all three dictatorships rounded up enemies of the state, real or imagined, at will, to be thrown into their nation's dungeons after sham trials or simply executed on the spot. The

A woman at a bazaar in Tripoli, Libya, 2002

repression wasn't limited to individuals but often extended to entire tribes or ethnic groups. Certainly the most notorious case was Saddam Hussein's Anfal campaign against Iraq's ever-restive Kurdish minority in 1988. Before that pogrom was over, between fifty thousand and one hundred thousand Kurds had been killed, while hundreds of thousands more were turned out of their razed villages and forcibly relocated.

The state also had a very long memory, as Majdi el-Mangoush discovered growing up in Misurata. In 1975, two of his mother's relatives, both midlevel army officers, had joined in a failed coup attempt against Qaddafi. While both were executed, their deaths weren't sufficient to remove the stain on the Mangoush family name. (Testament to the enduring tribal nature of Libya, Majdi's mother was also of the Mangoush clan and already bore the family name before marriage.)

"It's not that we were directly persecuted because of it," Majdi, who is now thirty, explained, "but it was something officials would always comment on: 'Ah, so you're a Mangoush.' It meant the government watched you a little closer, that you were never viewed as completely trustworthy."

And in all three countries, there dwelled one group that was deemed wholly untrustworthy, one that almost always received the stick: Islamic fundamentalists. In Syria and Iraq, even identifying oneself as a Sunni or Shia could draw state suspicion, and in all three nations, the mukhabarat had a special brief to surveil conservative clerics and religious agitators. Subtlety was not a hallmark of these campaigns. When, in February 1982, a group of Sunni fundamentalists in Syria under the Muslim Brotherhood banner seized control of portions of the city of Hama, Hafez al-Assad had the place encircled with ground troops and tanks and artillery. In the ensuing three-week "Hama massacre," somewhere between ten thousand and forty thousand residents were killed.

But a perverse dynamic often takes hold in strongman dictators—and here, too, there were great similarities among Qaddafi, Hussein, and Assad. Part of it stems from what might be called the naked-emperor syndrome, whereby, in the constant company of sycophants, the leader gradually becomes unmoored from reality. Another is rooted in the very nature of a police state. The greater the repression of security forces, the further that any true dissent burrows underground, making it that much harder for a dictator to know where his actual enemies are; this fuels a deepening state of paranoia, which can be assuaged only through even greater repression and an even tighter security cordon around the strongman. By the 1990s, this cycle had produced a bizarre contradiction in Iraq, Syria, and Libya: the more the leaders promoted a cult of hero worship and wallpapered their nations with their likenesses, the more reclusive those leaders became. In Majdi el-Mangoush's case, despite living in a country whose total population was less than that of Indiana, not once in twenty-five years did he ever personally glimpse Qaddafi. This was precisely the same number of times he uttered the dictator's name in a disparaging way in public. "You would only do that with family, or with the most trusted of friends," Majdi explained. "If you were around others and wanted to say something at all critical, it was 'our friend.'"

There was another notable aspect to the posters and murals and mosaics of the dictators that appeared everywhere in Libya, Iraq, and Syria. In a great many of them, framing the image of a ruminating Qaddafi or a smiling Hussein or a waving Assad was the outline of their country's borders. Perhaps that juxtaposition was designed to impart a simple message—"I am the leader of the nation"—but it's possible that the artificial-state dictators were sending a message that was both more ambitious and more admonishing: "I *am* the nation, and if I go, then so goes the nation." Of course, that may have been just what many members of Misurata's Mangoush clan—celebrated enough to have their own namesake neighborhood, notorious enough to be permanently marked—were secretly hoping.

3

Azar Mirkhan
Kurdistan

IN EARLY 1975, as Laila Soueif, at Cairo University, continued to agitate for change, General Heso Mirkhan was about to be betrayed. Mirkhan was a chief lieutenant to Mustafa Barzani, the legendary warlord of the Iraqi Kurds, and over the previous year, the vastly outnumbered Kurdish fight-

ers, known as the Peshmerga, had waged a brutal guerrilla war against the Baathist government in Baghdad and
fought the Iraqi army to a standstill. Crucial to the Kurds'
success had been a steady flow of CIA-supplied weaponry,
along with Iranian military advisers, as Iran conducted a
U.S.-sponsored border war against Iraq. At the beginning
of March, however, the shah of Iran and Saddam Hussein
abruptly concluded a peace treaty to end their feud, and
Secretary of State Henry Kissinger ordered an immediate
cutoff of aid to the Kurds. In the face of an all-out Iraqi
offensive, Mustafa Barzani was airlifted out to end his days
in a CIA safe house in northern Virginia, but thousands of
other stranded Peshmerga fighters were left to their fate,
including Heso Mirkhan. With Saddam Hussein's soldiers
closing in, the general led his family in a frantic dash over
the mountains for sanctuary in Iran. Somewhere along the
way, his wife gave birth to another son.

"The treaty was signed on the sixth of March," Azar
Mirkhan, who is now forty-two, explained, "and I was born
on the seventh. My mother gave birth to me on the road, on
the border between Iran and Iraq." He gave a rueful little
laugh. "That is why my family has always called me 'the
lucky child.' Kurdish luck."

Indeed, it is hard to find any people quite as unlucky as
the Kurds. Spread across the mountainous reaches of four
nations—Iraq, Iran, Syria, and Turkey—they have always
regarded themselves as culturally apart from their neighbors
and have constantly battled for independence from those
nations they inhabit. The governments of these nations
have tended to view their reluctant Kurdish subjects with

both fear and distrust and have taken turns quashing their bids for independence. Those governments have also periodically employed the Kurds—either their own or those of their neighbors—as proxy fighters to attack or unsettle their regional enemies-of-the-day. Historically, when those feuds were brought to an end, so, too, was the Kurds' usefulness, and they were swiftly abandoned—as occurred in the 1975 "Great Betrayal."

While the number of rebellions and proxy wars that have occurred across the breadth of Kurdistan over the past century is almost impossible to count, the biography of Heso Mirkhan's commander in chief, Mustafa Barzani, provides something of a gauge. By the time of his death in 1979, the seventy-five-year-old Barzani had not only waged war against Turkey, Iran (twice), and the central government of Iraq (four times) but had somehow found the energy to also take it to the Ottomans and the British and a host of Kurdish rivals. Multiply Barzani's list by four—the Kurds of Syria, Iran, and Turkey have each had their own competing guerrilla groups and independence movements—and it all becomes a bit staggering.

Despite the fears of these governments that they might someday be confronted by an independent "greater Kurdistan," the truth is that the differences among the Kurds in these four countries now outweigh their similarities; these differences include dialect, political orientation, even dress. One thing they have in common, though, is a long-standing warrior tradition, and among the Kurds of northern Iraq, there is no more celebrated family of Peshmerga—literally translated as "those who face death"—than the Mirkhans.

Following their father, Dr. Azar Mirkhan and four of his nine brothers have undergone Peshmerga training; today, one brother, Araz, is a senior Peshmerga commander on the front lines. But the family has paid a high price for membership in the warrior caste. Heso, the patriarch, was killed in combat in 1983, while one of Azar's older brothers, Ali, met the same end in 1994.

But it hasn't been just the region's governments that have historically victimized the Kurds. In fact, few nations have brought the Kurds of northern Iraq more sorrow than the United States. After their role in the Great Betrayal of 1975, the Americans would again be complicit in the Kurds' suffering—if this time largely through silence—just a decade later.

By then, the United States' chief ally in the region, the shah of Iran, had been overthrown and replaced by the hostile Shiite fundamentalist government of Ayatollah Khomeini. Searching for a new partner in the region, Washington found one in their erstwhile Baathist foe, Saddam Hussein. With the Iraqi dictator once again at war with Iran, but this time against the Khomeini regime, the United States secretly funneled weapons to his bogged-down military, enabling Hussein to extend the Iran-Iraq conflict for eight years at a cost of over one million dead. By 1988, the Iraqi despot was so integral to the Reagan administration's realpolitik policy in the region that it simply looked the other way when Hussein launched the murderous Anfal campaign against his Kurdish subjects. A squalid new low was reached in March of that year, when Iraqi forces poison-gassed the Kurdish town of Halabja,

killing an estimated five thousand people. Despite over-
whelming evidence that Hussein was responsible for the
atrocity—Halabja would figure prominently in his 2006
trial for crimes against humanity—Reagan administration
officials scurried to suggest it was actually the handiwork
of Iran.

What finally ended the American arrangement with
Saddam Hussein was the Iraqi dictator's 1990 decision to
invade neighboring Kuwait, upsetting not just the Western powers but most of his Arab neighbors. Perversely,
that event very nearly led to yet another slaughter of Iraq's
Kurds under Washington's watch. Instead, it would eventually lead to their liberation, as well as mark the crucial
moment when the United States propelled itself headlong
into Iraq's sectarian and ethnic divides.

In the face of Hussein's belligerence, President George
H. W. Bush marshaled an international military coalition—
Operation Desert Storm—that swiftly annihilated the Iraqi
army in Kuwait, then rolled into Iraq itself. With Hussein's government appearing on the verge of collapse, Bush
encouraged the Iraqi people to rise up in revolt. Both of
Iraq's marginalized communities—the Shiites in the south
and the Kurds in the north—eagerly did so, only to see
the United States suddenly take pause. Belatedly conclud-
ing that Hussein's demise might play into the hands of a
still-hostile Iran, the Bush administration ordered American troops to stand down as the Iraqi army regrouped and
began a pitiless counterattack.

To forestall a wholesale massacre of the rebels they had
encouraged, the United States joined its allies in establish-

ing a protected buffer zone in Kurdistan, as well as no-fly zones in both northern and southern Iraq. That still left Saddam Hussein in Baghdad, of course, and ready to take his revenge at the first opportunity. While the Bush administration concluded there was little it could do to aid the geographically isolated Shiites in the south—they soon suffered their own Anfal-style pogrom—to protect the Kurds, they forced Hussein to militarily withdraw from all of Kurdistan. Taking matters a step further, in July 1992, the Kurdistan Regional Government, an autonomous union of Iraq's three Kurdish provinces, was established.

The Bush administration most likely regarded this Kurdish separation as a stopgap measure, to be undone once the tyrant in Baghdad had gone and the danger passed. The long-suffering Kurds of Iraq saw it very differently. For the first time since 1919, they were free from the yoke of Baghdad, and they had their own nation in all but name. While very few in the West appreciated the significance at the time, the creation of the Kurdistan Regional Government, or KRG, marked the first dismantling of the colonial borders that had been imposed on the region seventy-five years earlier, the de facto partition of one of the Middle East's artificial nations. Naturally, the effect of this would be most profoundly felt in Iraq. A country with a scant sense of national identity to begin with now stood divided. What's more, by effectively removing the 17 percent non-Arab Kurdish population from the Iraqi demographic pool, the minority status of its Arab Sunni rulers had deepened in those portions of Iraq that remained, while the majority status of its marginalized Shiites had increased. In just this way, in 1992, the West had helped construct a sectarian time bomb liable to go off if ever Saddam Hussein lost his grip on power.

More immediately, with the creation of the KRG, tens of thousands of members of the Iraqi Kurdish diaspora began abandoning their places of exile to return to their old homeland. In 1994, that included a nineteen-year-old college student, Azar Mirkhan, who had spent almost his entire life as a refugee in Iran.

4

Majd Ibrahim
Syria

BEFORE ITS DESTRUCTION, Homs was a pleasant enough place, a city of roughly eight hundred thousand in the flat interior of Syria's central valley, but close enough to the foothills of the coastal mountain range to escape the worst of the region's tremendous summer heat. It was never a spot where tourists tarried very long. Although Homs dated back to before Greek and Roman times, little of the ancient had been preserved, and whatever visitors happened through the town tended to make quickly for Krak des Chevaliers, the famous Crusader castle thirty miles to the west. There was an interesting covered souk in the old city and a graceful if unremarkable old mosque, but otherwise Homs looked much like any other modern Syrian city. A collection of drab and peeling government buildings dominated downtown, surrounded by neighborhoods of five- and six-story apartment buildings; in its outlying districts could be seen the unadorned cinder-block homes and jutting rebar that give so many Middle Eastern suburbs the look of an ongoing construction site, or a recently abandoned one.

Yet, until its demise, Homs had the distinction of being the most religiously diverse city in one of the most religiously mixed countries in the Arab world. Nationally, Syria is composed of about 70 percent Arab Sunni Muslims, 12 percent Alawites—an offshoot of Shia Islam—and a roughly equal percentage of Sunni Kurds; Christians and a number of smaller religious sects make up the rest. At the geographic crossroads of Syria, Homs reflected this ecumenical confluence, with a skyline punctuated not just by the minarets of mosques but also by the steeples of Catholic churches and the domes of Orthodox Christian ones.

This gave Homs a cosmopolitan flavor not readily found elsewhere—so much so that in 1997, the Ibrahims, a Sunni couple, thought nothing of putting their first child, five-year-old Majd, in a private Catholic school. As a result, Majd grew up with mostly Christian friends and a better knowledge of Jesus and the Bible than of Muhammad and the Koran. This didn't appear to bother Majd's parents at all. Although raised as Muslims, both were of the nominal variety, with his mother rarely even bothering to wear a head scarf in public and his father dragging himself to the mosque only for funerals.

Such secular liberalism was very much in keeping with

the new Syria that Hafez al-Assad sought to shape during his otherwise typically draconian thirty-year dictatorship, a secularism undoubtedly encouraged by his own religious minority status as an Alawite. After his death in 2000, the policy was carried on by his son Bashar, a bland and socially awkward London-trained ophthalmologist. Although Bashar had come to power largely by default—the Assad patriarch had been grooming his eldest son, Bassel, to take over until a fatal car accident in 1994—he proved adroit at projecting a softer, more modern face of Baathism to the outside world, as well as at navigating the tricky currents of Middle Eastern politics. While still publicly vowing to recover the Golan Heights taken by Israel in the 1967 Six-Day War, the younger Assad maintained a tacit détente with Tel Aviv, even pursuing secret negotiations toward a settlement. By gradually loosening Syria's hold on neighboring Lebanon—its troops had occupied portions of the country since 1976, and Damascus was a prime supporter of Lebanon's Hezbollah militia—Bashar was viewed increasingly favorably by the West.

And to a young Majd Ibrahim then coming of age, it increasingly appeared that it was the West where his nation's future lay. Like other middle-class boys in Homs, he wore Western clothes, listened to Western music, and watched Western videos, but Majd was also afforded a unique window onto the outside world. His father, an electrical engineer, worked at one of the best hotels in Homs, the Safir, and Majd—fascinated by the hotel, with its constant bustle of travelers—made any excuse to visit him as he went about his day. For Majd, the Safir was also a place of reassurance, a reminder that no matter what small deviations Syrian politics might take along the way, he would always be able to inhabit the modern and secular world into which he was born.

PART II

The Iraq War

2003–2011

5

Khulood al-Zaidi
Iraq

BY THE VERY early morning hours of April 3, 2003, advance units of the United States I Marine Expeditionary Force had completed their encirclement of Kut al-Amara, a low-slung provincial city of some four hundred thousand located one hundred miles down the Tigris River from Baghdad. A message was then sent to the commander of Iraqi forces in Kut commanding him to surrender his forces by 7:00 A.M.

When no reply was forthcoming, American forces launched a devastating assault. Throughout that day, the Marines methodically destroyed one Iraqi redoubt after another, their tanks and artillery on the ground complemented by close air support. By afternoon, the fight for Kut was essentially over, marking it as just the latest one-sided affair that had typified the invasion of Iraq begun two weeks before; at the cost of one American soldier dead and about a dozen wounded, the First Marines had killed an estimated two hundred enemy combatants and captured some two thousand more.

Of this battle for her hometown, Khulood al-Zaidi, then

Civilians ducking for cover amid artillery attack near Basra, Iraq, March 2003

twenty-three, heard a great deal, but saw nothing at all. There was a simple explanation for this. "Women weren't allowed out of the house," she said.

Before the invasion, Vice President Dick Cheney predicted that American troops would be "greeted as liberators" in Iraq, and his prediction was borne out in the streets of Kut on April 4. As the Marines consolidated their hold on the city, they were happily swarmed by young men and children proffering trays of sweets and hot tea. Finally permitted to leave her home, Khulood, like most other women in Kut, observed the spectacle from a discreet distance. "The Americans were very relaxed, friendly, but mostly I was struck by how huge they seemed—and all their weapons and vehicles, too. Everything seemed out of scale, like we had been invaded by aliens."

That sensation was no doubt reinforced by the extremely

Chaos in the streets during the fall of Basra, Iraq, April 2003

circumscribed life Khulood had led up until that time. As the second youngest of six children—three boys and three girls—born to a hospital radiologist and his stay-at-home wife, Khulood had a relatively comfortable middle-class childhood but, like most of the other girls in Kut, one that was both cloistered and highly regimented: off to school each day and then straight home to help with household chores, followed by more study. Save for school, about the only times Khulood ventured from the modest al-Zaidi home was for the occasional family outing or to help her mother and older sisters with the grocery shopping. In twenty-three years, she had left her hometown only once, a day trip to Baghdad chaperoned by her father.

Yet, in the peculiar way that ambition can take root in the most inhospitable of settings, Khulood had always been determined to escape the confines of Kut, and she focused her energies on the one path that might allow for it: higher education. In this, she had an ally of sorts in her father. Ali al-Zaidi was insistent that all his children, including his three daughters, obtain college degrees, even if the ultimate purpose of the girls' education bordered on the obscure.

"My father was very progressive in a lot of ways," she explained, "but even with him, going to college was never about my having a professional career. Instead, it was always the idea of 'Study hard, get a degree, but then find a husband and go into the house.'" She shrugged. "This was the Iraqi system."

In the autumn of 1999, Khulood entered the University of Wasit in Kut to pursue a degree in English literature. The expectation in her family was that, degree in hand, she might teach English at a local school for a few years, then marry and start a family. Khulood had rather different plans, though: with her English proficiency, she would go to Baghdad and look for work as an interpreter for one of the few foreign companies then operating in Iraq.

That scheme was sidetracked when, just three months short of her graduation, the Americans invaded. But this proved only a temporary hitch. While there continued to be sporadic fighting elsewhere by remnants of Saddam Hussein's Baathist government—given the Orwellian label of "anti-Iraqi forces" by the Bush administration—the few coalition troops who remained in Kut that spring and early summer felt secure enough to mingle free of body armor with residents and to patrol its streets in unprotected trucks. Those soldiers also quickly returned the city to something close to normalcy. The university was reopened after just a two-month interruption, enabling Khulood to obtain her bachelor's degree that August. The real work now was in rebuilding the nation's shattered economy and reconstituting its government, and to that end, a small army of foreign engineers, accountants, and consultants descended on Iraq under the aegis of the Coalition Provisional Authority, or CPA, the United States—led transitional administration that would stand down once a new Iraqi government was in place.

One of those who came was a thirty-three-year-old lawyer from Oklahoma named Fern Holland. A human rights adviser for the CPA, Holland had a special brief in the summer of 2003 that included developing projects to empower women in the Shiite heartland of southern Iraq. In September 2003, that mission took her to Kut and her first encounter with Khulood.

"I will always remember the first time I saw Fern," Khulood said. "She brought a group of us women together to talk about the work she wanted to do in Iraq. She was surprisingly young—this is easy to forget, because her personality was so strong—with bright blond hair and a very open, friendly manner. I had never met a woman like her. I don't think any of us in that room had."

What Holland told the women in the Kut meeting hall was no less exotic to them than her appearance. With the overthrow of Saddam Hussein, she said, a new Iraq was being established, one in which democracy and respect for human rights would reign supreme. What's more, to consolidate this new Iraq, everyone had a role to play, not least the women of Kut.

For Khulood, that talk struck with the force of epiphany. This was the moment she had been waiting for her entire life. Almost immediately, she began doing volunteer work on women's rights projects for Holland. "I had thought about these issues before, but under Saddam Hussein, they were like fantasies," Khulood said. "Now, I saw a future for myself." For the young Iraqi woman, there was never a question of who had provided that future. "Fern Holland changed my life."

For her part, Holland was perhaps less confident. From past experience working in conservative and male-dominated societies in Africa, she suspected that it would only be a matter of time—and probably a very short time—before the forces of tradition rose up in opposition to her work, so she had to set change in motion quickly. She also knew that, as an outsider, her role needed to be a limited one; what was required was dynamic local women to spearhead the effort, women like Khulood al-Zaidi.

The following month, Holland chose Khulood to be a representative at a national women's leadership conference, held under the auspices of the CPA. At that conference, Khulood received even headier news: she had been selected as part of a women's delegation that would soon travel to Washington to help draft the new Iraqi constitution. When word of this spread at the conference, it provoked a backlash. "A lot of the other women objected because I was so young," Khulood said. "Even I thought it was maybe too much. But Fern insisted. She told the other women, 'Khulood represents the youth of Iraq—she is going.' She was my biggest supporter."

On that November 2003 trip to Washington, the twenty-three-year-old fresh out of college met with a parade of dignitaries, including President George W. Bush. Upon her return, she was formally hired by the CPA to serve as an assistant manager of the Kut media office. It was a very long way for a young woman who, less than a year earlier, had imagined no greater future than finding interpreter work with a foreign company. "It was a very exciting time," Khulood said. "Because you could feel everything changing so fast."

But even as she entered the new world opened up to her by Fern Holland, Khulood was occasionally struck by a pang of doubt, a vague sense of bad premonition. It was rooted in a feeling she'd had on that day in November when she and the other women in the Iraqi delegation were ushered into the Oval Office to meet President Bush. "There was just something about his manner that I found odd. He seemed distracted, a bit cold, and would never really look any of us in the eye. I didn't tell this to the other women because they were all so excited to meet the president, but I remember thinking to myself, 'If this is the man who controls our future, I think we are in trouble.'"

6

Wakaz Hassan
Iraq

WAKAZ HASSAN IS saved from ordinariness by his eyes. In most every other way, the tall and gangly twenty-two-year-old would appear unremarkable, just one more face in the crowd—but so intensely dark and arresting are his eyes that one might initially think he was wearing mascara. But it's more than coloring. In his stare is a kind of mournful impenetrability that hints at the hard world he has seen.

Only eight years old in 2003, Wakaz seemed destined for an exceedingly normal life, even a prosaic one. The youngest of five children born to an Iraqi bank clerk and his wife, he spent his childhood in the drowsy farming community of Dawr, just fifteen miles down the Tigris River from Saddam Hussein's hometown, Tikrit. "All was very good there," he recalled. "Easy."

That changed with the American invasion. Long considered a Baathist stronghold by virtue of Hussein's origins there, Tikrit and its environs were a prime early objective of the invaders, with the city itself the target of intense aerial bombardments. By mid-April 2003, coalition troops occu-

Wakaz Hassan, twenty-two

pied the string of gaudy palace buildings erected by Hussein along the Tikrit riverfront and began conducting raids through the surrounding river towns in search of fugitive Baathist officials. The May 15 raid on Dawr netted thirty suspected Baathists—a startling number for such a small community—but the town was soon to yield up an even greater prize. In mid-December 2003, American troops discovered a spider hole on the northern edge of Dawr and pulled out Saddam Hussein himself.

Of all this, the young Wakaz had only the vaguest grasp. According to him, his family—Sunni, like most all residents of the Tikrit area—was not particularly religious, nor was it political in any way. He remembered hearing something about the mistreatment of Iraqi prisoners at an American-operated prison—clearly a reference to the Abu Ghraib scandal—and then there was the time American soldiers searched his family's home, but those soldiers were quite respectful, and the episode passed without incident.

"I know others had problems with the Americans," Wakaz said, "but my family, no. For us, we were really not affected at all."

What the Hassan family did blame the invaders for, at least in a general way, was the ensuing collapse of the Iraqi economy, a downturn that cost Wakaz's father his job at the Rafidain Bank. To support his young family, the Hassan patriarch used his savings to open a small sweetshop on Dawr's main street. "So yes, our life was definitely much easier before the Americans came," Wakaz conceded. "Even if it wasn't their fault directly, that is when everything became much harder."

Later, the Tikrit region became one of the chief battlegrounds in the Sunni insurgency against coalition forces, the northern point of the notorious Sunni Triangle. Ultimately, well over four hundred coalition troops would die in the province. In turn, the Americans would try to quell the violence through the so-called Sunni Awakening, a "hearts-and-minds" campaign that often meant pitting one local tribe against another. If that campaign succeeded—and it largely did—it also had the effect of rekindling ancient tribal animosities.

The young Wakaz Hassan would play no role in these swirls of violence that swept through the Tikrit basin in the mid-2000s—but it wouldn't stay that way forever.

7

Khulood al-Zaidi
Iraq

AS SHE STARTED her new job with the Coalition Provisional Authority in the autumn of 2003, Khulood remained unaware that the seeds of disaster for the American intervention had already been sown.

In their Iraqi war plans, the Pentagon had set down comprehensive blueprints detailing which strategic installations and government ministries were to be seized and guarded but seemed to have given little thought to the arsenals and munitions depots that Hussein had profligately scattered about the country. In one town and city after another, these storehouses were systematically looted, often under the gaze of coalition soldiers who had been given no orders to intervene.

The occupying authorities soon compounded this misstep. In a move now largely regarded as calamitous, one of the first actions taken by the CPA's administrator, Paul Bremer, was to disband the Iraqi military. Just like that, hundreds of thousands of men—men with both military training and access to weapons—were being put out of their jobs by the summer of 2003.

It may have been the edict immediately preceding that decree, however, that had the most deleterious effect. Under the terms of CPA Order 1, senior Baath Party members were summarily dismissed from government positions and placed under a lifetime public-employment ban. In addition, employees in the upper echelon of all government institutions were to be investigated for Baathist affiliations. As critics pointed out, tens of thousands of apolitical Iraqi professionals—a group that included Khulood's radiologist father, Ali al-Zaidi—had been compelled to join the party in the 1990s as part of a "recruitment drive" by Saddam Hussein; now these teachers and doctors and engineers were at risk of being disenfranchised.

But the effects of Order 1 stretched far beyond those Baathists directly dismissed. In Iraq, as in much of the rest of the Middle East, government offices operated on an elaborate patronage system in which most every employee, from senior staff down to the steward who brought refreshments to visitors, owed their jobs to the head man; as might be expected in a still-tribalistic culture, that man—almost invariably a Baath Party member during Saddam Hussein's reign—usually handed out those jobs to members of his extended family or clan. What the firing of some eighty-five thousand Baathists actually meant, then, was the cashiering of countless more people and the instant impoverishment of entire clans and tribes. It was a broad array of those Iraqis disenfranchised in 2003—an amalgam of tribes and Baathists and ex-soldiers—who would be in the vanguard of the civil war that was to break over the nation in 2004. And less than a decade later, it would be the Sunni component of these same excluded groups who would rally to the banner of ISIS.

Under the weight of these blunders, perhaps the most remarkable feature of the Iraqi occupation is that it didn't blow up sooner. A taste of what was to come occurred in August 2003, when the United Nations headquarters in Baghdad was destroyed by a truck bomb, killing twenty-two, including the UN's special representative for Iraq, Sérgio Vieira de Mello. That was followed by a steady escalation in attacks against coalition forces. By the beginning of 2004, CPA officials perceived a deepening hostility toward even their most noncontroversial initiatives, so much so that Fern Holland began to worry. As she wrote in an e-mail to a friend in late January: "We're doing all we can with the brief time we've got left. It's a terrible race. Wish us luck. Wish the Iraqis luck."

On March 8, 2004, the new provisional Constitution of Iraq was signed. The clause that set a goal of having 25 percent of future parliamentary seats held by women was largely credited to the behind-the-scenes lobbying of Fern Holland.

The following afternoon, a Daewoo containing three CPA civilian employees was traveling along a provincial highway when an Iraqi police pickup truck pulled alongside. With a blast of automatic gunfire, the car was sent careering across the highway before stalling on the shoulder; the men in the police truck then clambered out to finish off their victims with assault rifles. All three of the

Daewoo's occupants were killed in the fusillade, marking them as the first CPA civilians to be murdered in Iraq. That included the driver and presumed target of the attack, Fern Holland.

With Holland's murder, a sense of trepidation spread among the thousands of CPA personnel scattered across Iraq. "We were all in a state of shock, of course," Khulood al-Zaidi said, "but I think we were also waiting to see what it meant, if it had been an attack on Fern in particular or if this was going to be something larger."

The answer came very soon. In tandem with the growing Sunni insurgency in central Iraq, through the first months of 2004, a radical Shiite cleric in Baghdad, Moktada al-Sadr, had been demanding a withdrawal of all coalition forces from the nation. In early April, Sadr unleashed his militia, the Mahdi Army, in an effort to bring that withdrawal about through a series of well-coordinated attacks on military and CPA installations. Kut's turn came on April 5, when some two hundred Mahdi militiamen began attacking the CPA compound.

Khulood spent hours trapped in the CPA media office, as the coalition forces assigned to guard the compound returned fire. Finally, a CPA supervisor turned to Khulood. "If you are not afraid," he said, "you should just go."

With two other local workers, Khulood managed to thread her way out of the compound and, dodging down side alleys, to escape. With the CPA compound subsequently abandoned, she remained in hiding as the Mahdi militiamen who now controlled Kut searched for any local CPA employees left behind. Even after American forces retook the city, Khulood remained so frightened she didn't leave her family's home for two weeks.

The Mahdi uprising radically altered the flow of events in Iraq. Both Sunni and Shia militias now sharply increased their attacks against coalition forces, marking the true beginning of the Iraq War. Despite this, the CPA went ahead with their program of effectively ceding control of Iraq to a new central government. In May, the last of the foreign civilians based in Kut began withdrawing, and within two months, the whole of the local CPA infrastructure was placed under the authority of the new Baghdad government.

For a time, this did seem to calm passions in Khulood's hometown, enough so that she vowed to continue the women's rights initiatives begun by her murdered mentor. That autumn, she helped found a small nongovernmental organization called Al-Batul, or Virgin. Its goals were modest. "Kut has a small Christian population," Khulood explained, "so my idea was to bring Christian and Muslim women together to work on projects that were important to both communities. It was mainly to teach the women how to defend their rights, to show them that they didn't always have to obey what men said."

But in the deepening sectarianism spreading across Iraq, Sunni and Shia militants alike increasingly viewed the Christian community as the infidels within; in turn, terrified Christians were beginning to abandon the nation in droves, an exodus that would eventually reduce their numbers in Iraq by more than two-thirds. Further, the only possible source of funding for an endeavor like Al-

Khulood al-Zaidi, thirty-six

Batul was from the foreign occupiers, enabling militants to denounce it as a front in the service of the enemy. Almost immediately, Khulood began receiving anonymous threats for continuing her work on "American issues," threats that escalated to the point where she was denounced by name in a local newspaper.

The memory of that time caused Khulood, now thirty-six, to become somber, reflective. "I can see now that I was quite naive, that I didn't take the situation as seriously as I should have. But my feeling was that I was only working on things that might give women a better life, it was not political in any way, so how was I a threat?"

In October 2004, the Al-Batul office in Kut was shot up. Undeterred, Khulood rented a second office, only to have it looted. That January, while attending a human rights training seminar in Amman, the capital of neighboring Jordan, she received a warning: if she resumed her work in Kut, she would be killed. She remained in Jordan for three months, but in April 2005—a year after the death of Fern Holland and with the fighting in Iraq now spiraling into sectarian war—Khulood finally slipped back to her hometown.

She recognizes now that this decision bordered on the foolhardy. "It was just very difficult for me to give up on this dream I had for Iraq," Khulood said, recalling how Holland told her that "to bring change, it takes people with courage, that sometimes you have to push very hard. Well, I didn't want to die, but Fern had, and I think I held on to this hope that if we kept trying, maybe things would improve."

Shortly after returning to Kut, Khulood went to the local police station to file a report about her looted office, only to be treated dismissively. A more ominous note was struck when she met with one of her old Al-Batul colleagues. "Why did you come back here?" the woman asked. "Everyone knows you're working for the American embassy." Her colleague's accusation came on the heels of a call summoning Khulood to the local militia headquarters. "That's when I finally saw there was no chance for me in Iraq, that if I tried any longer, they would surely kill me."

8

Laila Soueif
Egypt

AS KHULOOD WAS planning her escape from Iraq in April 2005, Laila Soueif was escalating her opposition to the Egyptian dictatorship of Hosni Mubarak.

By then, Laila and her husband, Ahmed Seif, had been Egypt's most celebrated political dissident couple for well over a decade, serving as constant nuisances to the Mubarak government. Since his release from prison in 1989, Ahmed had become the nation's preeminent human rights lawyer, the champion of an eclectic array of defendants in politically motivated cases that included leftist university professors, Islamic fundamentalists, and—in a nation where homosexuality remains effectively illegal—members of Cairo's gay community. When I first met him that autumn, Ahmed was involved in perhaps the most controversial case of his career, defending a group of men accused of complicity in a 2004 hotel bombing in the Sinai Peninsula that left thirty-one dead.

For her part, and even while retaining her mathematics professorship at Cairo University, Laila had gained a reputation as one of Cairo's most indefatigable "street" leaders, the veteran of countless protest marches against the regime. Part of what drove her was a keen awareness that, as a member of the Cairene professional class, she enjoyed a freedom to dissent that was all but denied to Egypt's poor and working class.

"Historically," she said, "that bestowed a degree of immunity—the security forces really didn't like to mess with us, because they didn't know who in the power structure we could call up—but that also meant we had a responsibility, to be a voice for those who are silenced. And being a woman helped, too. In this culture, women just aren't taken that seriously, so it allows you to do things that men can't."

But Laila was also quite aware that her activism—and the government's grudging tolerance of it—fit neatly into the divide-and-rule strategy that Hosni Mubarak had employed since assuming power in 1981. In the past, Egyptian governments had been able to gin up bipartisan support when needed by playing the anti-West, anti-Israel card, but Anwar Sadat had traded that card away by making peace with Israel and going on the American payroll. The new strategy under Mubarak consisted of allowing an expanded level of political dissent among the small, urban educated elite, while swiftly moving to crush any sign of growing influence by the far more numerous—and therefore, far more dangerous—Islamists.

The regime was greatly aided in this effort in the mid-1990s when a radical Islamist group, Al-Gamma'a al-Islamiyya, launched a terror campaign, culminating in a horrific knife and machine-gun attack on tourists at Luxor's

Hatshepsut Temple in November 1997 that left sixty-two dead. In response, Egyptian security forces launched a scorched-earth campaign against Al-Gamma'a and its alleged sympathizers across the country, killing hundreds and imprisoning tens of thousands more. That bloody episode sent an implicit warning to Mubarak's liberal opponents that, if their agitation for political reform got out of hand, what waited in the wings was not parliamentary democracy but religious fanaticism. Also hearing that warning was the American government, by then subsidizing the Egyptian regime to the tune of some $2 billion a year.

In Laila's estimation, what finally caused this strategy to fray was the launch of the second Palestinian intifada, or uprising, against Israel in September 2000. With most Egyptians of all political persuasions holding to the conviction that their government had sold out the Palestinians with the 1979 peace treaty with Israel, Mubarak was suddenly powerless to muzzle pro-Palestinian demonstrations lest he be seen as an even greater lackey of the Americans. "For the first time," Laila explained, "we began organizing openly and publicly without taking any permission from the government and without taking cover under any of the so-called legitimate political parties. And what was the government going to do about it? This established the pattern—you don't wait for permission, you don't look for an existing political party to take you in, you just organize—that we used many, many times afterward."

In short order, street protests became a constant feature of Egyptian life. Even more deleterious from the regime's point of view, fury over the Palestinian situation galvanized opposition groups from across the political spectrum to march and work together.

With this new dynamic in place, the last thing Hosni Mubarak needed was another reminder to the Egyptian people of his fealty to Washington—but then came the United States' decision to invade Iraq.

While astute enough to oppose that invasion in public, and to engage in high-profile diplomacy to try to head it off, Mubarak wasn't able to escape its fallout. In the eyes of many Egyptians, after twenty-two years of taking lucre from the Americans, the dictator was simply too much their puppet to make a show of independence now. That cynical view only hardened as the war in Iraq dragged on and the daily body count mounted. From 2002 through early 2005, some of the largest antiwar demonstrations in the Arab world were taking place in the streets of Cairo, and Laila Soueif was on the front lines in nearly every one of them. "Of course, on the overt level, it was to protest what was occurring in Iraq," Laila said, "but this also reflected the failure of Mubarak."

At the same time, the dictator did himself few favors with a series of domestic initiatives that further inflamed the opposition. Grooming his son Gamal as his successor, in February 2005, Mubarak engineered a rewriting of the constitution that, while ostensibly allowing for direct presidential elections, actually rigged the system so as to make domination by his political party all but perpetual. In presidential elections that September, Mubarak won a fifth six-year term with nearly 89 percent of the vote, after having arrested the only notable candidate to stand against him, Ayman Nour. Under mounting pressure at home and abroad, he reduced his interference in the November 2005 parliamentary elections, only to see the Muslim Brotherhood, an Islamist party still officially banned, take an unprecedented 20 percent of the seats.

By late 2005, when I spent six weeks traveling through Egypt, growing contempt for the government was evident everywhere. To be sure, much of that antipathy derived from the nation's economic stagnation and from the corruption that had enabled a small handful of politicians and generals to become fabulously rich—the Mubarak family financial portfolio alone was reported to run into the billions—but it also had a strong anti-American component, and pointed up a profound disjuncture. At the same time that Egypt was regarded in Washington as one of the United States' most reliable allies in the Arab world, due in no small part to its continuing entente with Israel, over the course of scores of interviews with Egyptians of most every political and religious persuasion, I failed to meet a single one who supported the Israeli peace settlement, or who regarded the American financial subsidies to the Mubarak government as anything other than a source of national shame. As Essam el-Erian, the deputy head of the Muslim Brotherhood, bluntly told me, "The only politics in Egypt now are the politics of the street, and for anyone to work with the Americans is to write their political death sentence."

It was during this time of ferment that the three children of Laila Soueif and Ahmed Seif, who previously had shown little interest in activism, began to have a change of heart about politics. The first to make the evolution was their son, Alaa, a pioneering Egyptian blogger, and it happened when he accompanied Laila to a protest march in May 2005.

"He had become very interested in citizen journalism," Laila said, "so with all the street actions surrounding the constitution and Mubarak running again, he had begun coming down to cover the demonstrations—not to participate, just to report on them."

But the protest on May 25 was a very different affair. Waiting in ambush were government-hired thugs, or baltagiya who immediately charged at the demonstrators to beat them with fists and wooden staffs. Perhaps recognizing the well-known protester in their midst, the goons soon fell on Laila.

"Well, this was something new," she said, "for them to punch a middle-aged woman, and when my son saw that, he jumped in to help me." For his trouble, Alaa was beaten up as well. "He had some toes broken, so we went to hospital, and it was only later that we discovered we were the lucky ones. After we left, the baltagiya began pulling the clothes off women and beating them in their underwear. This was something they did a lot later on, to humiliate, but that was when it began and when Alaa joined the protests. The girls became involved later—Mona got pulled in with the judges' independence movement, and then for Sanaa, it was the revolution—but for Alaa, it started in 2005."

Laila Soueif is a tough, unsentimental woman, and if she harbored any pride—or, in light of what was to come, regret—over her children's turn to activism, she didn't let on. "I never tried to dissuade them. Even if I had wanted to—and I probably did at times—I didn't. That kind of thing is useless. They're not going to listen to you anyway, so you just get into fights."

Sitting in her Cairo apartment in March 2016, Laila's sister, the novelist Ahdaf Soueif, had a rather more contemplative view when pondering what has happened to her sister's family in recent years. "I don't think anyone sets out to be a martyr, to be a sad cause," Ahdaf said. "I think you start down a path, and something happens, and then you go a little further and something else happens, and eventually you reach a point where you don't see any way back, you can only keep going. I think that's what happened to Laila and Ahmed, and I think that's what happened to their children, too."

9

Majdi el-Mangoush
Libya

IT WAS AROUND this time that Majdi el-Mangoush joined onlookers on a sidewalk in his hometown, Misurata, to witness an incredible sight.

Along Tripoli Street, one of the city's main thoroughfares, a municipal work crew with a cherry picker was methodically taking down the posters of Muammar el-Qaddafi that hung from every lamppost.

It was part of an attempt by the Libyan dictator to put a kinder, gentler face on his government. While ostensibly directed at the Libyan people, the campaign was really meant for Western consumption.

In the days leading up to the invasion of Iraq, there had been talk in President George W. Bush's administration that once Saddam Hussein was dispatched, Qaddafi would be next on the American chopping block. Once that invasion got under way in March 2003, the Libyan dictator hurried to make nice with the Americans. Toward closing off two long-standing points of contention with Washington, he offered a settlement over his country's role in the 1988 bombing of Pan Am Flight 103 over Lockerbie, Scotland—without explicitly admitting guilt, the Libyan government agreed to set aside $2.7 billion in compensation to the families of the 270 victims—and began quietly dismantling his nation's fledgling program for chemical, biological, and nuclear weapons. Even more quietly, Libyan intelligence agents shared dossiers with their American counterparts on suspected Al Qaeda operatives and other Islamic fundamentalists in the region. Extending this rehabilitation campaign to the home front, the goal was to create at least the illusion of political liberalization, and one aspect was to remove some of the tens of thousands of posters and billboards of "the Leader" that wallpapered the nation.

But Qaddafi soon thought better of the whole egalitarian makeover, especially once the United States restored full diplomatic relations with his government in 2006. While officially a response to the abandonment of the Libyan unconventional-weapons program, certainly a contributing factor to this détente was a recognition that, amid the deepening quagmire of the Iraqi misadventure, there was not going to be any grand American crusade against the region's other dictators—which also meant that Qaddafi could abandon the trappings of domestic reform. "It was just a bit of theater," Majdi said. "Nothing really changed, and after a few months, I don't think anyone even remembered it."

But that day hadn't yet arrived when the cherry picker made its way down Misurata's Tripoli Street. Majdi was still observing the spectacle when an elderly man emerged from a nearby alley.

For a long moment, the old man stared slack jawed in amazement at the sight before him. He then rushed over to one of the discarded posters, removed a shoe, and—in a gesture of insult common throughout the Arab world—began beating it against Qaddafi's likeness amid a torrent of curses.

A municipal worker came over to ask what he was doing.

"The bastard's gone at last, no?" the old man asked. "There's been a coup?"

When the worker set him straight, the man stammered out an explanation for his behavior—he'd been very ill lately, given to fits of lunacy—and then hurried away.

10

Khulood al-Zaidi
Jordan · United States · Iraq

KHULOOD DID NOT flee Iraq alone. She crossed back into Jordan with her next-eldest sister, Sahar, and they were joined in Amman a few months later by their father and oldest sister, Teamim. Choosing to stay on in Iraq were Khulood's three brothers, along with her mother, Aziza. By summer 2007, Khulood was especially worried about Wisam, her youngest brother. "The war then was at its worst," she said, "and young men were just being taken from the streets. I called Wisam all the time. I told him there was no future for him in Iraq, that he had to come out, but he was very softhearted and said that he needed to stay to take care of our mother."

One evening that September, as Wisam and a friend walked along a Kut street, a car pulled up alongside, and someone with an assault rifle killed them both in a burst of gunfire. "He was twenty-five," Khulood said softly. "Some people say he was killed because of the work I was doing, but I hope that isn't true."

A few months after Wisam's murder, Khulood faced a

new ordeal when, working for an NGO, she rebuffed the demands of a corrupt but well-placed Jordanian business-man looking for kickbacks. He was the wrong person to cross. Shortly after, she was ordered to leave Jordan. Fac-ing almost certain death if forced to return to Iraq, Khu-lood turned to the United Nations High Commissioner for Refugees (UNHCR) for emergency resettlement in a third country.

Among the more unlikely possibilities for resettlement was the United States. In 2008, American troops were still embroiled in an Iraqi civil war, and the Bush administra-tion had strict caps in place (albeit recently loosened) on the number of Iraqis to be given refuge; to let in all those who had fled the country—and there were an estimated half mil-lion displaced Iraqis in Jordan alone—would belie its talk-ing point that the corner had finally been turned in the war. In light of the grave danger Khulood faced, however, the UNHCR placed her in its own special program, reserved for only the most vulnerable of refugees, and for those in this pool, the Americans had a spot available. In July 2008, Khulood boarded a plane bound for San Francisco.

It's hard to imagine a more extreme transition, from the cramped, tumbledown apartment she had shared with her father and two sisters in Amman to a pleasant one-bedroom in San Francisco, but with the help of a group of solicitous new friends, Khulood soon reveled in her transformed life. "Just to have the freedom to go wherever I wanted, and to not think something bad might happen to me. And I don't mean just the war. For a woman to travel alone in Iraq—maybe it happened in Baghdad, but never in Kut, and so some days I would just take a bus or the metro for hours. It was something I had never really imagined before."

The move produced moments of cultural dissonance. One of Khulood's new friends urged her to smile more. "You're in California now. Everyone here smiles all the time."

The young woman from Kut found this suggestion quite baffling. In Iraq, women were taught to wear a stern face in public and to avoid eye contact with men so as to not be mistaken for prostitutes, but Khulood, eager to fit into her new American home, dutifully practiced smiling in front of her bathroom mirror. She soon suspected she was doing something wrong, because whenever she displayed her new demeanor on the streets of San Francisco, it drew unwanted attention, especially from homeless men. Her friend hastily amended her advice. "You don't need to smile at *everyone*."

Another change was her career horizons. In Iraq, Khulood studied English because it seemed to offer the greatest chance at future freedom for a young woman, but in the United States, the opportunities were endless. "After one year, I would get my green card, and then I could apply for scholarships to study whatever I wanted. I became very ambitious, thinking of all the things I might want to do."

The one continuing source of worry was for her divided family back in Iraq and Jordan. While she knew those in Kut wouldn't leave, Khulood was desperate to release her father and sisters from their limbo existence in Amman, and, soon after reaching San Francisco, she started the paperwork to have them join her.

Three months later, Khulood received both good and bad news. Her two sisters were approved for resettlement. Their father, however, was rejected. Khulood's sisters remained in Jordan while the family appealed the decision, but Ali al-Zaidi was rejected again.

By February 2009, seven months after Khulood's arrival in San Francisco, there was still no progress in the effort to win resettlement for her father. It was then she made a fateful decision: she would return to Jordan and work on his case there.

"My friends in San Francisco couldn't understand it," she recalled. "Why, when you have a new life here, why would you ever go back?" Khulood grew thoughtful for a moment, as if still struggling for an answer. "But how to explain my culture to them? In Iraq, family is the most important thing, you can never turn away from it, so how could I and my sisters enjoy this nice life in America but leave our father behind? We could never live with the shame of that. So I went back."

In Amman, Khulood tirelessly pursued any angle she could think of to win her father's exit, petitioning for settlement not just in the United States but also in a half dozen European nations. Nothing worked.

Worse, Khulood had walked herself into legal limbo. As she had been warned before leaving San Francisco, under the stipulations of American immigration law, refugees awaiting the permanent status of a green card cannot leave the country for longer than six months. By returning—and staying—in Jordan, Khulood had lost her refugee classification. Now, along with the part of her family that she had brought out of Iraq, Khulood was stranded, equally unable to go home or to a third country, hostage to the whim of a state—Jordan—that was anxious to shed her.

11

Majdi el-Mangoush
Libya

IN THE SUMMER of 2009, Majdi el-Mangoush spent several days hiking through the Jebel Akhdar, or Green Mountain, an expanse of forested peaks and verdant valleys and plunging rivers on Libya's northeastern coast. At the age of twenty-two, Majdi had never seen a rushing stream before, let alone a true forest, and he quickly decided the Jebel Akhdar was the most beautiful place he had ever seen. He was accompanied on the trip by his best friend, Jalal al-Drisi.

That he knew Jalal at all was actually the by-product of a disappointment in Majdi's life. As the youngest of Omar and Fatheya el-Mangoush's six children, Majdi had been raised in a close-knit family that valued education. All three of his older sisters and two brothers had attended Libya's better universities, and certainly the expectation was that Majdi would follow in their footsteps. Instead, by narrowly failing to get high enough marks on the national exam to gain admission to the top-tier schools, the youngest Mangoush sibling had been forced to find an alternative. In the

Majdi el-Mangoush, thirty, in front of a tank in Libya

autumn of 2008, Majdi became a cadet at the national air force academy, based in Misurata, toward earning a degree in communications engineering. There, he met and became fast friends with Jalal al-Drisi, a twenty-one-year-old cadet from the eastern Libyan city of Benghazi.

As often seems the case with best friends, Majdi and Jalal were a study in contrasts. Whereas Majdi was stocky, even given to a slight chubbiness, Jalal was wiry and quick on his feet. And where Majdi was soft-spoken and tended to shyness, Jalal was gregarious and witty, always ready with the irreverent joke or the elaborate prank. What the two shared was a fascination with science and gadgetry. By coincidence, the friends had something else in common: a slight black mark against their family names in the eyes of the state. For Majdi, this stemmed from the purported involvement of two male relatives in a coup attempt in 1974. In

Jalal's case, he was the son of a senior police officer who, in the wake of bloody antigovernment protests in Benghazi in 2006, was briefly imprisoned for dereliction of duty.

Over the course of their first year at the air force academy, Jalal frequently spent his weekend leaves at the Mangoush family home in Misurata. To reciprocate that hospitality, the Drisi family invited Majdi to spend part of the 2009 summer break with them in Benghazi. The historical division of Libya between west and east, between Tripolitania and Cyrenaica, was evidenced in Majdi's description of that trip. "It was my first time to the east," he said, "and in Misurata, we were raised with this idea that the easterners were a bit primitive, far more tribal. I was actually surprised by how normal it was."

In Libyan tradition, the Drisi family royally feted their young guest. In between forcing obscene amounts of food on Majdi, they ferried him to local areas of interest, with the trek to Jebel Akhdar being the highlight.

"I think it was that trip, seeing the forest for the first time, that drew me so much to nature," Majdi said. "In Misurata, it was mostly just palm trees, bushes, but to walk in a real forest . . . well, it was a very special experience."

By the autumn of 2010, the two cadets were looking forward to their third and final year at the academy, and planning their futures. Majdi intended to find work with one of the Western technology companies that had set up shop in post-sanctions Libya, while Jalal hoped to study more advanced aviation weaponry in Europe. Instead, the friends were about to become pawns in one of the strangest—and most tragic—side stories of the bloody Libyan revolution.

12

Majd Ibrahim
Syria

THE AMERICAN INVASION of Iraq was initially quite worrisome for Bashar al-Assad. After a long period of tension, Syrian relations with the mercurial and dangerous Saddam Hussein had warmed recently, and even though his nation was not on President Bush's original "axis of evil" hit list, the Syrian dictator was naturally nervous that an American occupation army on his frontier could make him an attractive next target. But just as with Muammar el-Qaddafi in Libya, by the late 2000s, Assad could be quite confident that he had nothing to fear from a flailing United States.

Not that this confidence translated into greater political freedom for the Syrian people. Just as in his father's day, Assad's subjects lived in constant fear of internal security agents and a network of government-sanctioned thugs, or shabiha. So pervasive was this spying apparatus—or at least the fear of it—that politics wasn't so much a delicate subject in most Syrian homes as no subject at all.

"I can never remember my father saying anything about the regime, good or bad," Majd Ibrahim said. "And I never remember any of my relatives or neighbors doing it either. When it came to the state, the most anyone would criticize was maybe the corrupt traffic policeman at the corner. You just didn't talk about that stuff with anyone."

Because of his liberal upbringing, Majd experienced a shock when he left his Catholic school at the end of the ninth grade and transferred into a state high school. His modern and secular ways often estranged him from his more Islamist-minded classmates, and the instruction was abysmal. But high school is a bad time for a lot of people, and Majd's life brightened considerably upon graduating in the summer of 2010. While failing to obtain the high marks on the national exam that would have enabled him to pursue one of the "higher" professions—engineering or medicine—he did sufficiently well to enter Al-Baath University in Homs that autumn to pursue a degree in hotel management.

This was undoubtedly a better fit for Majd regardless. The handsome, outgoing young man had a natural charm that enabled him to develop a quick rapport with most anyone, joined to an intense curiosity about the larger world beyond Homs. With his degree in hand, he envisioned a future at one of the luxury hotels in Damascus—they "represented one of the best ways to advance," he said, "to have a good life."

But there was another feature of his hometown that Majd had probably scarcely given thought to in his short life: in almost every way, Homs truly was the crossroads of Syria. Located near the midpoint of the highway between the nation's two largest cities, Damascus and Aleppo, Homs was also the eastern terminus of the highway linking Syria's interior to its coastal provinces. Just as significant, it was the hub of the nation's gas and oil-refinery industry—quite logically, since the pipelines leading from the oil and natural gas fields in the eastern deserts passed directly through the city on their way to the coast. If all this served to make Homs a prosperous town, it also meant that, in the event of a war, it was a place all sides would fight furiously to control.

By the time Majd started at Al-Baath University, that war was just months away.

BY THEN, THE United States had largely extricated itself from the Iraqi morass. A phased withdrawal of military forces begun by the Bush administration in 2008 continued under the new administration of Barack Obama.

That withdrawal was far more extensive than originally envisioned. For the rocky road that still lay ahead in Iraq, the Bush administration had wanted to retain a limited fighting force in the country for the foreseeable future. Those plans were scuppered when the Shiite-dominated government of Nouri al-Maliki refused to grant American personnel immunity from local prosecution for any future crimes or misdeeds they might commit. Without that grant of immunity, in the fall of 2008, the Bush administration announced that virtually all American combat forces would leave Iraq by 2011. The disastrous consequences of that decision would not be evident until the spring of 2014, when a handful of ISIS gunmen swept into western Iraq to scatter the hapless Iraqi army before them.

In the meantime, the American intervention in Iraq continued to have an unsettling effect in the region, in the form of a growing public disenchantment with its Western-allied leaders and a growing militancy among traditional Islamists. The eruption finally came with Mohamed Bouazizi's suicide in Tunisia and the rapid spread of protests across the region in 2011.

Even with the Bouazizi case, however, there was one small detail, barely noted at the time, which might have caused the hopeful to take pause. During the fourteen days that the Tunisian fruit seller lingered before succumbing to his burn injuries, some of those who wished to promote his martyrdom added the provocative detail that the policewoman with whom Bouazizi had his public altercation slapped him. The allegation was almost certainly untrue—no eyewitness to the incident reported seeing such a thing, and the policewoman strenuously denied it—but it suggested that already elements were twisting the Bouazizi narrative to fit their own political goals, and these goals were not toward democracy or liberalism but toward conservatism and a rejection of those "Western ideas" that would ever allow a policewoman to have the temerity to strike a man.

PART III

Arab Spring

2011–2014

13

Laila Soueif
Egypt

LAILA HAD BEEN involved with Egyptian politics for far too long to believe all the talk about the protest being held in Tahrir Square on January 25, 2011. "It's not going to be a demonstration," one young activist told her. "It's going to be a revolution." She understood the man's excitement. Only days earlier, street protests after the self-immolation of the fruit-and-vegetable vendor in Tunisia had forced the longtime Tunisian strongman Zine el-Abidine Ben Ali from power. Throughout the Arab world, rebellion was in the air. But this was Egypt. Laila expected news conferences and solidarity committee meetings, perhaps some paper reforms, certainly not insurrection. She even joked about it. She was attending an educational conference the day before the demonstration, and when an organizer asked if she would be returning the next day, she replied, "Well, tomorrow we're having a revolution, but if the revolution ends early, yes, I'll be here."

The following day, as Laila approached Tahrir Square, she realized this indeed was something altogether different from

Demonstrator at Tahrir Square, Egypt, 2011

the toothless Egyptian protests of the past. Until now, the Cairene activist community had considered a protest successful if it drew several hundred demonstrators, with any topping a thousand participants regarded as exceptional. In Tahrir Square on January 25, the crowd was at least fifteen thousand, and Laila soon heard about the many thousands more who had converged on different rallying points around Cairo and in other towns and cities across Egypt. In Tahrir, as elsewhere around the nation, the stunned security forces simply gave way before the onslaught, stood impotently by as the emboldened crowds' calls for reform gave way to open demands for Hosni Mubarak's fall.

It wasn't merely the numbers that convinced Laila this was a radical departure from past protests. "In Tahrir, I met people who'd come in from all over northern Egypt. Some

Demonstrators at Tahrir Square, Egypt, 2011

had traveled hundreds of kilometers, and they were determined that they weren't going home until they'd toppled
Mubarak."

The protests continued over the next two days, until,
on January 28, Laila concluded that they truly did have
a revolution on their hands. That morning, she and some
friends traveled to the Imbaba neighborhood in northwest
Cairo to join a group intending to march on Tahrir, only to
be met by a wall of soldiers in riot gear. After dispersing the
protesters, the soldiers pursued them into Imbaba's narrow
alleyways, firing tear gas as they went.

"That was a very stupid mistake," Laila explained. "These
are small alleys where people are practically living in the
street, so that just brought down Imbaba. It became a fixed
battle between the troops and the residents, and there was

absolutely no moving those people. They were going to break down these soldiers and torch the police stations, or die trying."

The battle for Imbaba continued late into the afternoon. Laila, having become separated from her friends, decided to walk to downtown alone. It was an eerie journey. The streets were deserted, but everywhere in the growing dusk things were burning: cars, barricades, police stations. Echoing off the surrounding buildings came the sound of gunfire, some single shots, others the sustained bursts of assault rifles. With darkness falling, Laila finally emerged onto Ramses Street, a major thoroughfare in central Cairo.

"And suddenly, this huge crowd of demonstrators appeared," she recalled, "running down Ramses. They had just broken through the police cordons, and they were running to get to Tahrir. One young man saw me standing there, and he came over and hugged me—he'd obviously seen me before, in Tahrir—and said, 'I told you we would have a revolution!' And that was the moment when I knew it was true, and that we would be victorious."

Over the next week, both the size and the militancy of the demonstrations grew, but so did the harshness of the government's response, with soldiers and the police increasingly trading tear gas for live ammunition. On February 1, a defiant Mubarak took to the airwaves vowing never to leave Egypt—"On its soil I will die"—and the following day there came the bizarre spectacle, dubbed the Battle of the Camel, when scores of state-sponsored thugs astride horses and camels attacked those encamped in Tahrir Square with riding crops and whips.

The following day, Ahmed Seif's law center was raided by the military police, and he and dozens of others were hauled off for questioning at the headquarters of military intelligence. For two days, Ahmed was interrogated by a variety of officers, but he would have reason to recall one encounter in particular. It came on the morning of February 5, when the chief of military intelligence, a colorless general named Abdel Fattah el-Sisi, going about other business, happened to stride past Ahmed and several other prisoners. In an impromptu lecture, Sisi warned his captive audience that they should all respect Mubarak and Egypt's military leadership and that, once released, they should go home and forget Tahrir Square. When Ahmed, forgoing respectful silence, retorted that Mubarak was corrupt, the general's haughty manner swiftly changed. "He became angry; his face became red," Ahmed recalled a few years later to *The Guardian*. "He acted as if every citizen would accept his point and no one would reject it in public. When he was rejected in public, he lost it."

Upon his release that day, Ahmed stopped by his home for a change of clothes and then immediately returned to Tahrir Square.

The sense that the regime was coming apart became increasingly palpable. Across Egypt came reports of army units refusing orders to fire on demonstrators, and in Tahrir Square, television cameras captured images of soldiers embracing the protesters and sharing cigarettes with them.

On February 11, the clock finally ran out on Hosni Mubarak. After submitting his resignation, the president and his immediate family boarded a plane and fled to their

palatial retreat in the Red Sea resort town of Sharm el
Sheikh. At the news, all of Egypt erupted in celebration,
and nowhere more so than in Cairo's Tahrir Square.

But among a small handful of Egyptians, joy was
already tinged with a note of disquiet, especially when it
was announced that a group of senior military officers, the
Supreme Council of the Armed Forces, or SCAF, would
serve as an interim government until elections were held.
One of those who worried was Laila Soueif.

"In the last few days of Mubarak," she said, "when we
could see what was coming, I and some of the other inde-
pendents, we tried to talk to all the different political factions. 'Seize power. Don't wait for permission. Just seize
power now before the military steps in.' And everyone said,
'Yes, of course, that's a good idea. We'll organize a meeting
to talk about it in a couple of days.'" Laila shook her head,
gave a bitter little laugh. "But maybe it was asking too
much. Maybe we simply couldn't do it at that point. People
needed to feel they had won. Not us, the politicos, but all
these millions of people who had come down to the street.
They needed a time to feel victorious." She sighed and then
fell silent for a moment. "I don't know. To this day, I don't
know. But I think that was our critical moment, and we
lost."

14

Majdi el-Mangoush
Libya

EARLY ON THE morning of May 9, 2011, Majdi el-Mangoush said good-bye to his companions at the isolated farmhouse on the outskirts of Ad Dafiniyah and headed alone into no-man's-land. His destination was his hometown of Misurata, some ten miles to the east.

As he walked, the sound of gunfire grew in intensity, and there was the occasional rumble of distant artillery explosions, but between the light wind and the rolling-hill topography of the Misurata coastal shelf, it was quite impossible for Majdi to determine how close any of it was or even its direction. He tried to bear in mind something he'd picked up in basic training, that the most worrisome noise on a battlefield wasn't gunshots but rather a soft popping sound, like the snapping of fingers. This was the sound the air made as it rejoined behind a bullet, and you only heard it when a bullet passed close to your head.

In the right front pocket of his pants, Majdi carried his military identification card, listing him as a third-year cadet in the Libyan Air Force. If he was stopped by the rebels, this card in itself was unlikely to cause him problems; by now, three months into the conflict, countless government soldiers had deserted, and the fact that Majdi was from Misurata would certainly lend credence to his explanation that he was trying only to go home. The Thuraya satellite phone in his left pocket was a very different matter, though. With the severing of Internet and cell phone reception in Libya, the Thuraya had become the standard mode of communication for regime operatives in the field, and if the rebels discovered Majdi's—sure to be found in the most cursory of searches—they would inevitably conclude he was coming into Misurata as a spy. Under those circumstances, summary execution was probably the most merciful outcome he could hope for.

If this was the scenario that had played out, Majdi's executioners would have had it exactly right. The soft-spoken twenty-four-year-old air force cadet was returning to his hometown on a secret mission: to ascertain where in Misurata the rebel leadership was based, and to then relay that information to Libyan military intelligence so those leaders could be assassinated.

On that day, it would have been difficult to find anyone among Libya's six million citizens with less of a grasp of what had happened in the country over the previous three months than Majdi el-Mangoush. Making his ignorance all the more remarkable, he hadn't spent that time in some remote desert outpost but rather at the very epicenter of the Libyan civil war.

On their sprawling compound in southwestern Misurata that January, Majdi and his fellow air cadets had watched

the news of the upheavals in Tunisia and Egypt in astonish-
ment. In Majdi's case, his knowledge of the spreading chaos
abroad was augmented by the time he spent with his family
and civilian friends on weekend breaks. Still, neither he nor
any of his classmates connected that tumult to their situation in Libya, much less imagined it might spread there.

Then, on the evening of February 19, a Saturday, the
cadets heard a series of crackling sounds coming from
within the city. At first, they thought it might be firecrack-
ers, but the sounds intensified and drew nearer, until the
students realized it was gunfire. Soon they were ordered
to assemble at the drill ground, where they were informed
that all leave had been canceled. By then, the watchtowers
that ringed the compound—usually empty or occupied by
a single bored sentry—were manned by squads of soldiers
with mounted machine guns.

"That's when we knew something big had happened,"
Majdi recalled, "because this was unlike anything we'd seen
before. But still, no one would tell us what was going on."

Majdi hoped he would get an explanation when classes
resumed the next morning, but when the civilian instruc-
tors failed to show up, that potential source of outside
information was cut off, too. All that day and into the
next, the gunfire beyond the walls continued sporadically,
the sound drawing nearer at times, only to recede, intense
exchanges followed by long periods of quiet. Throughout,
Majdi stayed in the constant company of his best friend
at the academy, Jalal al-Drisi, and in the bizarre news-free
environment in which they now existed, the two young
men tried to puzzle out what was happening.

A measure of clarity finally came on February 22, when Muammar el-Qaddafi, clad in an olive-drab robe, addressed the nation. In what almost instantly became known as the Zenga Zenga speech, the dictator laid blame for the social unrest then spreading across Libya on foreign conspirators and "rats," and he vowed to purify Libya "inch by inch, house by house, room by room, alley by alley"—*zenga zenga* in Qaddafi's pronunciation of the Arabic word for *alley*— "person by person."

No sooner did Qaddafi's address end than the gunfire in Misurata spiked. "It was like the security forces had been awaiting orders for what to do," Majdi said. "After the speech, they just opened up everywhere."

What didn't change, though, was the cadets' peculiar quarantine, purportedly in danger from elements outside the compound walls whose goals remained mysterious and kept within those walls by soldiers who clearly didn't trust them. As the days passed and the unseen gun battles raged, the students lounged around their barracks or wandered the vast compound wondering what was to become of them. It was virtually all Majdi and Jalal could talk about. "We would sit together for hours and go over every little detail, every clue we had picked up," Majdi said. " 'What did it mean? Did it mean anything?' But sometimes it got to be too much. We had to stop. We had to talk about football or girls, anything to distract us."

Their peculiar limbo ended on the night of February 25, when soldiers of the elite Thirty-Second Brigade suddenly appeared on the base. Announcing that they had come from Tripoli to "rescue" the cadets, the commandos ordered the students to pack their things and run to a gathering point at the edge of the compound where buses were waiting.

Perhaps the Thirty-Second's hallowed reputation didn't extend to their logistical personnel, for to transport the 580 cadets, someone had decided to order up just two buses. With both vehicles filled to bursting, the excess students were crammed wherever they might fit in the brigade's jeeps and armored cars, and then the convoy trundled into the night for the long journey to Tripoli.

For a regime in desperate need of a positive photo-op, the air force cadets from Misurata proved a boon. The following afternoon, they were led into a Tripoli assembly hall where the better spoken among them were hustled before television cameras to give profuse thanks to the Thirty-Second Brigade and to "the Leader" for their rescue, even if just who they had been rescued from remained unclear. To provide a pleasing backdrop during these testimonials, the rest of the cadets, including Majdi, were instructed to crowd in, smile, and wave the small Libyan flags they had been given. With his core shyness, Majdi stayed at the back of the crowd and was surprised by how many of his flag-waving classmates competed to mug in front of the cameras, until a thought came to him. "They were doing that so their families back home would see them and know they were still alive. I wish I had figured that out sooner, because I hadn't talked to my family since the start of the fighting, and they had no idea where I was."

Beyond effecting their "rescue" from Misurata, the regime in Tripoli didn't really seem to know what to do with its young charges either. Bused to a vacant military high school compound on the southern outskirts of the city, the cadets were billeted in barrack halls and empty classrooms but barred from leaving or having any contact with their families. That edict was enforced by armed soldiers posted at the gates.

But the confines of the Tripoli high school were a good deal more porous than those of the air force academy, and from their minders the cadets gradually learned something of the conflict that had befallen their nation. Although the unrest was fomented by criminal gangs and foreign mercenaries in the hire of Libya's Western enemies, they were told, enough misguided segments of the population had joined in to cause its spread. By the beginning of March, this foreign-spawned criminality was most intense in Misurata and Benghazi, Majdi's and Jalil's hometowns, and both those cities were now pitched battlegrounds.

Provided with this narrative, Majdi was not altogether surprised when, in mid-March, Western alliance warplanes began appearing over Tripoli to bomb government installations. To the contrary, those strikes seemed merely to confirm that the nation was being attacked from beyond. Naturally, the situation also caused both Majdi and Jalal to worry about the fate of their hometowns and wonder which of their friends might have been seduced into joining the traitors' ranks. "That's something we talked about a lot," Majdi said. " 'Oh, Khalid was always a little crazy; I bet he's gone with them.' "

As the rumors from Misurata and Benghazi grew steadily worse—by early April, there were reports that whole swathes of the cities had been destroyed—life inside their gilded cage became that much more excruciating for Majdi and Jalal. Their predicament also gave rise to a moment of gallows humor.

One afternoon, as the two friends dejectedly wandered the high school grounds, a passing army officer took notice of their manner and drew them up. "Why so grim, boys?" he asked. "It's all going to work out."

Falling into conversation with the cadets, the officer finally asked where they were from. Upon hearing Misurata and Benghazi, the officer shook his head, whistled through his teeth. "Well, like I said, it's all going to work out—but just maybe not for you guys . . ."

The air force cadets seemed gradually to win the trust of the regime, enough for one large group to be transferred to a military base in mid-April to begin training on missile-guidance systems. Neither Majdi nor Jalal were selected for this mission, however, and their stay at the high school dragged on. Then one day in early May, Majdi ran into an old acquaintance at the barracks. The acquaintance, Mohammed, was now a military intelligence officer, and he wanted to talk to Majdi about Misurata. The two chatted for some time, with Mohammed asking about different locations in the city and if the young cadet might know who the town's "civic leaders" were. Majdi thought nothing of the conversation, but one afternoon a few days later, he was called to headquarters.

There, an officer informed Majdi that he had been selected to join the cadets undergoing missile-guidance training; the jeep that would transport him to the base was leaving immediately. So hurried was his departure that Majdi didn't even have time to say good-bye to Jalal.

But the jeep driver didn't take him to the army base. Instead, he followed the Tripoli ring road to the coastal highway and then turned east. Majdi had no idea where he was going, and the driver wasn't in a talkative mood.

By early evening, they had reached Ad Dafiniyah, the last town before Misurata and the farthest limits of government control. There, Majdi was led into a small farmhouse, where he was told someone wanted to speak to him on the phone. It was Mohammed, the military intelligence officer.

As Mohammed explained, the air force cadet had been chosen for a "special patriotic mission": Majdi was to slip into Misurata and find out who the rebel leaders were and where they lived. Once he had done this, he would pass the information to a liaison officer secreted within Misurata, a man named Ayoub. To make contact with Ayoub, Majdi was given a Thuraya satellite phone and a number to call.

Upon hearing all this, Majdi had two thoughts. One was about his friends at home; ever since hearing about the scale of fighting in Misurata, he assumed that some of his friends must have joined the other side. If he carried out this mission, it might very well result in their deaths.

The other thought was of a conversation he'd had with Jalal just days earlier. His friend had awoken in a despondent state of mind, explaining that he'd had a terrible dream, and it took Majdi some time to coax out the details. "I dreamt that you and I were sent to fight in Misurata," Jalal finally revealed, "and that you were killed."

But any hesitation swiftly passed. In his goldfish-bowl existence in Tripoli, Majdi had heard only what the regime wanted him to hear, and if he didn't believe all of it, he believed enough of it to want to help defeat the foreigners and their followers who were destroying Libya, even if this included people he knew. Perhaps most of all, he just wanted the limbo to end. For nearly three months, he had been cut off from both his family and the outside world, and he simply wanted something—anything—to happen. So he agreed and early the next morning set off into no-man's-land.

Majdi's memory of that journey is vague. He doesn't remember how long it took; he estimates that he walked for about three hours, but it could have been shorter or twice as long. Only one moment sticks out in his mind. About half-way across no-man's-land, Majdi was suddenly filled with a sense of joy unlike anything he had ever experienced before.

"I can't really describe it," he said, "and I've never had a feeling like it since, but I was just so happy, so completely at peace with everything." He fell silent for a time, groping for an explanation. "I think it's because I was in the one place where I was out from the shadow of others. I hadn't betrayed my friends yet, I hadn't betrayed my country yet—that is what lay ahead—so as long as I stayed out there, I was free."

15

Majd Ibrahim
Syria

LIKE MAJDI EL-MANGOUSH in Libya, Majd Ibrahim was at first merely an outside observer of the deepening turmoil in the Arab world in early 2011. The Syrian dictatorship made no attempt to conceal the revolts in Tunisia and Egypt from its people, and indeed spoke of them openly with a certain smugness. "We have more difficult circumstances than most of the Arab countries," President Bashar al-Assad grandly informed *The Wall Street Journal* on January 31, "but in spite of that, Syria is stable. Why? Because you have to be very closely linked to the beliefs of the people."

Shortly after that interview, however, Syria's state-controlled media went silent on the whole topic. Certainly, there was scant mention when, in early March, demonstrators took to the streets of the southern Syrian city of Dara'a to protest the arrest and reported torture of a group of high school students for writing antigovernment graffiti on walls. "I heard about what happened in Dara'a through social media," Majd said, "from Facebook and YouTube."

It was from the same venues that Majd learned of a

solidarity protest, called the Day of Dignity, that was to take place in front of the Khalid bin al-Waleed Mosque in downtown Homs on March 18. Heeding the admonitions of his parents, Majd stayed well away from that rally, but he heard through friends that hundreds of demonstrators had shown up, watched over by a nearly equal number of police officers and state security personnel. It was a shocking story to the eighteen-year-old college student; Homs had simply never experienced anything like it.

And that demonstration was tiny in comparison with the next, held a week later. This time, the protesters numbered in the thousands. Majd, figuring there was safety in numbers amid the throngs of onlookers, managed to get close enough to hear their demands: for political reform, greater civil rights, a repeal of the state-of-emergency edict that had been in place in Syria for the previous forty-eight years.

On March 30, Assad delivered a speech to the Syrian parliament, carried live by state television and radio outlets. While protests had now spread to a number of Syrian cities, they were still largely peaceful, with dissenters calling for changes in the regime rather than for its overthrow. As a result—and with the assumption that the regime had learned something from the recent collapse of the Tunisian and Egyptian governments and the widening chaos in Libya—many expected Assad to take a conciliatory approach.

That expectation was also based on Assad's personality. In the eleven years he had ruled the nation since the death of his father, the unassuming doctor had adopted many trappings of reform, and with his attractive young wife, the British-born Asma, put a pleasing, modern face on the Syrian autocracy. In a case of exquisitely poor timing, that very month, *Vogue* magazine was running a gushing profile of the Syrian First Lady, entitled "A Rose in the Desert," focusing on Asma's work with children and her snappy fashion sense.

Behind the charm offensive, however, little had truly changed; Syria's secret police were still everywhere, and the "deep state"—the country's permanent ruling class of bureaucrats and military figures—remained firmly in the hands of the Alawite minority. The Alawites, along with many in Syria's Christian minority, feared that any compromise with the protesters was to invite a Sunni revolution and, with it, their demise.

After offering vague palliatives about future reform, Assad instead used his parliamentary speech to accuse the troublemakers in the streets of aiding the "Israeli enemy" and to issue a stern warning. "Burying sedition is a national, moral, and religious duty, and all those who can contribute to burying it and do not are part of it," he declared. "There is no compromise or middle way in this." In keeping with a tradition begun during his father's reign, Assad's speech was repeatedly interrupted by members of the parliament leaping to their feet to shout out their undying love and gratitude to the president.

In Majd's memory, a kind of uneasy quiet fell over Homs after Assad's address. There were still scattered protests about town, watched over by phalanxes of heavily armed security forces, but it was as if no one was quite sure what to do next—each side fearful, perhaps, of leading the nation into the kind of open warfare then roiling Libya.

The interlude ended abruptly on April 17, 2011. That evening, as reported by Al Jazeera, a small group of demonstrators, maybe forty in all, were protesting outside a mosque in Homs when several cars stopped alongside them. A number of men clambered out of the cars—presumably either local plainclothes police officers or members of the largely Alawite shabiha—and then proceeded to gun down at least twenty-five of the protesters at point-blank range.

It was as if gasoline had been thrown on a smoldering fire. That night, tens of thousands of demonstrators took over Clock Tower Square in downtown Homs, and this time, the police and shabiha took to the roofs and upper floors of the surrounding buildings to shoot down at them. "That is when everything changed," Majd said. "Where before it was protests, from April 17 it was an uprising."

But it was an uprising with a distinct and ever-worsening pattern. As protesters started to be killed almost every day, their funerals the next day became rallying points for more protesters to take to the streets; the evermore brutal response of the security forces at these gatherings then created a new round of *shaheeds*, or martyrs, ensuring greater crowds—and more killing—at the next funerals. By early May, the cycle of violence had escalated so swiftly that the Syrian army came into Homs en masse, effectively shutting down the city.

"Nobody trusted the local security forces," Majd recalled, referring to the vast apparatus of mukhabarat and uniformed police who traditionally held sway in Syrian towns. "But everyone liked the soldiers coming in. Even I did, because we believed they had come to protect the people and stop the killing. And it worked. The army had tanks and everything, but they didn't use them, and very soon the killing ended."

After just a short time, however, the regime withdrew the bulk of its military forces from Homs in order to deploy them on "pacification" operations elsewhere—and with the army no longer able to provide order, the mukhabarat began distributing heavier weapons to the semiofficial shabiha. The city swiftly fell back into bloodletting. Around Homs, vigilante forces set up roadblocks and conducted raids into neighborhoods now controlled by the rebels. Throughout the summer, the fighting continued, with different factions of pro- and anti-regime gunmen taking control of ever more sections of the city.

Then matters took an even more sinister turn. In this most religiously mixed of Syrian cities, suddenly people began turning up dead for no other discernible reason than their religious affiliation. In early November 2011, according to a Reuters account, gunmen stopped a bus and murdered nine Alawite passengers. The next day, at a nearby roadblock, Syrian security forces, seemingly in retaliation, led eleven Sunni laborers off to be executed. All the while, a terror campaign of kidnappings and assassinations targeted the city's professional class, leading many of them to go into hiding or flee.

The fighting also had a surreal inconstancy. Some districts saw ferocious battle, even as, in others, shops stayed open and the cafés were full. Majd Ibrahim's Waer neighborhood fell into this latter category, and by carefully monitoring the news for reports of specific conflagrations occurring in the city, the college student was able on most days to navigate the two-mile journey to his hotel management classes on the Al-Baath University campus. By February 2012, however, the fighting had become so indiscriminate that the university announced it was temporarily closing. At the same time, rumors were circulating through Homs that the Syrian Army would be returning in force, this time to put down the rebellion once and for all.

"That's when my parents decided to send me to Damascus," Majd explained. "With the university closed and the fighting about to get worse, they felt there was no reason for me to stay—and it was going to become especially dangerous for young men." When Majd left for the Syrian capital in early February, he passed a seemingly endless line of army transport trucks, tanks, and artillery pieces parked on the shoulder of the highway just outside Homs. The next day, the Syrian army moved in.

By then, ten months into the fighting, Homs had won the nickname the Capital of the Revolution. It was about to earn a new one: the Stalingrad of Syria.

16

Majdi el-Mangoush
Libya

THE FIRST LIVING soul that Majdi el-Mangoush saw upon reaching Misurata's western outskirts was a young boy, perhaps eight or nine, playing in the dirt. The homes all around were deserted and shell-pocked, but then he noticed a car parked in the shadow of a farmhouse wall.

"Is your father here?" Majdi asked the boy. "Will you take me to your father?"

At the farmhouse, Majdi met the boy's father, a man in his thirties, who was both astonished and deeply suspicious of this stranger emerging from no-man's-land. Majdi repeated his cover story: that he had deserted from the regime and was trying to reach his family. He was helped in this subterfuge by his surname, for everyone in Misurata knew of the Mangoush clan. The man's wariness eased off, and he offered Majdi a lift into town.

As much as he'd heard about the fighting in his hometown, Majdi was unprepared for the reality. Since late February 2011, Misurata had been increasingly under siege by government forces, its residents becoming almost wholly dependent on whatever food and medical supplies could be brought in by sea. All the while, the army had rained down artillery shells, while its soldiers fought the rebels alley by alley, person by person, just as Qaddafi had promised. The siege abated somewhat with the advent of Western alliance air strikes in late March, but the damage done to the city was astonishing. Everywhere Majdi saw buildings blasted by tank shells or scorched by fire, destruction so great that in some places he couldn't even tell which street or intersection they were passing.

The man from the farmhouse dropped Majdi off at his family's home. "I just came through the front door," he recalled. "The first person I saw was my sister. And then there were my sister-in-law and my brother's children." At the memory, Majdi blinked back tears. "It had been three months. I thought I would never see them again."

Majdi spent the rest of that day in reunion with his family. He learned that after his father became seriously ill, his parents had gone out aboard a medical evacuation ship to Tunisia. He also learned that the list of local "traitors" to the regime didn't just consist of old friends but extended to his own family; in fact, for several weeks, his oldest brother, Mohammed, had secreted a group of deserting air force helicopter pilots in a back room of his own home. Everyone, it seemed, had joined the revolution, and they were now committed, after all Misurata had suffered, to see it through to the finish.

At some point during this family gathering, Majdi briefly excused himself to go to his old bedroom. There, he took the Thuraya from his pocket and hid it on a shelf behind a bundle of bedding. "I didn't know what I was going to do yet," he said. "I just knew that I had to hide that phone."

Over the next week, the returned son of Misurata wandered about his ruined city, meeting up with friends and learning of those who had been wounded or killed in battle. In the process, he came to see that everything he had been told and had believed about the war was a lie. There were no criminals, there were no foreign mercenaries—at least not among the rebels. There were only people like his own family, desperate to throw off dictatorship.

But this realization placed Majdi in a very delicate spot. Ayoub, his intelligence contact, surely knew of his arrival in Misurata and was expecting him to report in. Majdi briefly entertained the idea of simply discarding the Thuraya and going on as if nothing had happened, but then he thought of the repercussions that would befall his family if the regime won out in the end. Or what if the rebels uncovered the Qaddafi spy cell in the city and his name surfaced?

Faced with these possibilities, the air force cadet came up with a far cleverer—and more dangerous—plan. In mid-May, he presented himself to the local rebel military council and revealed all. As Majdi well knew, for a would-be spy to throw himself on the mercy of the enemy in wartime is never a good bet—the rebels' most expedient path would be to imprison or execute him—but against this outcome, he made a bold offer.

The next morning, Majdi finally contacted Ayoub, his regime handler, and agreed to meet two days later in a vacant apartment building downtown. No sooner was that meeting under way than a group of rebel commandos burst in with guns drawn and quickly wrestled both men to the ground. Majdi and Ayoub were then placed in different cars for transport to prison. By the time the rebel military council announced that it had captured "two regime spies" in Misurata, Majdi was already back at his family home.

Although the sting had come off perfectly, there were apt to be other regime operatives in Misurata aware of Majdi's assignment, making it risky for him to move about the city. He took advantage of the moment to slip off to Tunisia to visit his parents.

For Majdi, the contrast of Tunisia—modern, peaceful— was yet another journey into bewilderment. "It was so quiet, so relaxed," he recalled, "that it took me some time to believe it was real."

Majdi might easily have stayed on in Tunisia—it's certainly what his parents wanted—but after a few weeks, he grew restless, gnawed by a sense that his role in his country's war wasn't complete. "I think part of it was a kind of revenge. I had been with the army, but they had lied and manipulated me. And, of course, the war wasn't over yet; people were still fighting and dying. I told my parents I had no choice. I had to go home."

Back in Misurata, Majdi immediately became active with a local rebel militia, the Dhi Qar Brigade, for the march on Qaddafi's redoubt in Tripoli. Before he could be deployed there, however, the government forces in the capital collapsed, and the dictator and his remaining loyalists retreated down the coast to Sirte, Qaddafi's tribal homeland district. There, surrounded and with their backs to the sea,

Libyan refugees at the Tunisian border near Ben Gardane, 2011

they waged a desperate last stand. For a month, Majdi's unit held a stretch of the Sirte bypass highway, shelling regime strongholds and engaging in the occasional firefight whenever the trapped soldiers tried to break out. As elsewhere in the Libyan war—as in most wars, frankly—combat in Sirte was a curiously desultory affair, moments of intense action followed by long stretches of tedium, and to Majdi it seemed this rhythm might continue indefinitely.

Instead, it ended very suddenly on October 20, 2011. That morning, a fierce firefight erupted in the western part of Sirte, punctuated by a series of air strikes from Western coalition warplanes; from his perch on the bypass road, Majdi saw enormous plumes of fire and dust rising up from the bombs exploding around the city. Around 2:00 P.M., there came another concentrated flurry of small-arms fire from the western suburbs, one that lasted about twenty

minutes, before all fell quiet. Initially, Majdi and his comrades thought it meant that Qaddafi's men had surrendered,
but there soon came even better news: the dictator himself
had been captured and killed. "We all cheered and hugged
each other," Majdi recalled, "because we knew it meant the
war was over. After all that killing—and after forty-two
years of Qaddafi—a new day had finally come to Libya."

With the fighting at an end, Majdi returned to Misurata and transferred to a militia unit involved in tasks more
suited to his gentle character: he joined an ambulance crew
ferrying the more severely war-wounded from Misurata's
hospitals to the airport for advanced medical treatment
abroad. He greatly enjoyed this work, which he felt showed
tangible evidence of recovery after so much death and dev-
astation, and it fortified his optimism about the future.

Then one December day at the Misurata airport, Majdi
received a visitor. He was Sameh al-Drisi, the older brother
of his friend Jalal, and he had traveled the five hundred
miles from Benghazi to ask a favor.

17

Majd Ibrahim
Syria

MAJD SPENT FOUR months in Damascus as street battles raged throughout his hometown, and even though the atmosphere in the capital was tranquil—disconcertingly so—he was eager to get back to his family and his studies. Finally in May 2012, the situation in Homs had sufficiently calmed to allow the university to reopen.

Majd had kept in regular contact with his parents and friends during his Damascus stay, so he knew that the fighting in Homs had been centered in the Baba Amr neighborhood south of downtown. He'd been told that the damage was extensive, but he wasn't at all prepared for the reality. "We drove past it on the day I got back," he recalled, "and . . . well, it was just gone. Everything was gone. I remember thinking—trying to find something positive, you know?—everyone should come see this. If people saw Baba Amr now, maybe it would be a lesson. They would understand how terrible war is."

The naiveté of that notion soon became obvious; within weeks of Majd's return, the battle for Homs started up in earnest again. This time, the regime was targeting the insurgents in the Khalidiya neighborhood, and because the army's main artillery staging ground was next to the Waer district, it meant shells passed directly over the Ibrahim family's apartment building at all hours.

"When they went overhead," Majd said, "it was like the air was sucked away. I don't know how else to describe it, but you felt it in your lungs. It was hard to breathe for maybe a half minute afterward, like all the oxygen was gone."

The fighting in Homs raged on through the summer of 2012, with the Syrian military methodically targeting one rebel-held neighborhood after another, their ground-troop assaults backed up by tanks, artillery, and helicopter gunships. Just as in the earlier fighting, though, the middle-class neighborhood of Waer remained an oasis of comparative calm. Majd attributed it to Waer's diversity; with its mixed population of Sunnis, Alawites, and Christians, none of the rebel militias could truly control the enclave—and if the militias weren't there in force, the overextended Syrian army couldn't be bothered.

By the autumn of 2012, that began to change. On the streets of Waer, Majd noticed more and more young men toting weapons, and of those who wore insignia, by far the most common was that of the Free Syrian Army, or FSA. The militiamen also took notice of Majd. Of perfect combat age at twenty, he found his daily ventures to the university growing ever more stressful as the gunmen demanded to know whom he was allied with or taunted him for not "joining up."

In response to the growing tension in Waer, the Ibrahims began renting a "shelter home"—a safety measure that many of the city's more affluent residents were adopting. By now, so many families had fled Homs that furnished apartments sat empty throughout the city. Contacting one such family that had left for Damascus, Majd's father arranged to rent their apartment in an outlying neighborhood for use whenever trouble cropped up in Waer. At first, the Ibrahims decamped to their shelter home only occasionally, but by early 2013, their flights had increased in frequency to two or three times a week. Their greatest concern was for the safety of their eldest son at the hands of the militias.

"Most of them were just guys from the neighborhood who'd managed to get their hands on some guns," Majd explained. "I knew a lot of them—I'd grown up with them—so that was good. But more and more were coming in from the outside, and those guys were tough. A lot of them were survivors of the battles in Baba Amr and Khalidiya. They were suspicious of everyone, and you just never knew what they were going to do."

Adding another unsettling element to the mix, a lot of the fighters were on drugs, habitually popping an amphetamine called Captagon that could keep them alert for days, counteracted by an antianxiety drug called Zolam to bring them down.

Of all the various armed groups that had pitched up in Waer—and many were little more than neighborhood self-defense committees—the Free Syrian Army spurred a particular disdain in Majd. In contrast to what many in American foreign policy circles were professing to see in the FSA at the time—secular progressives who, if supported, might lead Syria to democracy—what Majd saw was a bunch of opportunists and cowards.

"At least the guys in the Islamist groups had some beliefs and discipline," he said, "but most of the FSA in Waer were just young guys who wanted to walk around with guns and scare people. And the funny thing about that is they were the ones who scared very easily. If another group came into their area, they would just turn around and join that group."

One day, Majd came upon a young FSA commander he'd come to know quite well, and who was never without a cigarette in his mouth, sitting dejectedly and cigarette-less. When Majd asked why he wasn't smoking, the militiaman explained that he wasn't FSA anymore. His unit had been taken over by an Islamic group, and his new leader had decreed that smoking was haram, or forbidden.

18

Majdi el-Mangoush
Libya

THE FAVOR THAT Sameh al-Drisi asked of Majdi was help in locating his younger brother, Jalal. It was December of 2011, the Libyan revolution had been over for two months, but the last time anyone in the Drisi family had heard from Jalal was in May. That communication was a short phone call from the Tripoli high school where the air force cadets had been sequestered, and it came just days after Majdi left for his spying mission to Misurata.

Taking leave from his job ferrying the war-wounded to medevac planes at Misurata airport, Majdi set out in search of his lost friend with a tenacity that bordered on obsession. Returning to Tripoli, he spent weeks tracking down some of their former academy classmates and, from them, was able to piece together at least part of the mystery. It led Majdi directly back to Misurata.

In May 2011, Jalal had been among a group of some fifty cadets at the Tripoli high school who were assembled and told they were being sent to assist in back-base operations outside Misurata. As was explained to them, this meant they would follow behind frontline troops as they advanced on the rebels in the city, checking for old booby traps and guarding communication and supply lines. Instead, the cadets were used as bait there, sent out over open ground to be shot and shelled at, while the regime's more seasoned soldiers sat back to observe where the enemy fire was coming from. As one cadet after another fell on this suicide mission, Jalal and two of his comrades managed to reach an outlying farm, where they begged an old farmer to take them south, away from the battlefield; instead, the farmer betrayed the students and delivered them to internal security forces, who in turn delivered them right back to the army. After a round of beatings, the three were sent back to their suicide squad.

But that was as far as the tale went. Shortly after, Jalal's two companions had made a second escape attempt—this time successfully—but by then, Jalal had been moved to a different part of the front.

This set Majdi off on a new search. He finally found another former classmate who completed the story. One day in June, a small group of the cadets—Jalal and others who had managed to survive that long—were bivouacked along a farm road on Misurata's southern outskirts when an officer drove up and called the students over for a situation report. In that same moment, a missile from an unseen Western alliance warplane or drone blew apart the officer's car, instantly killing him and most of the cadets standing nearby. Jalal al-Drisi was not among them. When the missile struck, he was sitting beneath a tree some fifty yards away, but it was there that an errant piece of shrapnel found him, tearing off the top of his head. His surviving companions buried Jalal's spilled brain beneath the tree but put his corpse in a truck with the other dead for transport to some unknown cemetery.

"Of course, I was reminded of the dream he'd had," Majdi said. "Yes, we'd both gone to Misurata to fight, but it was he who died."

For most people, this might have meant an end to the search, but not Majdi. Recalling the time he had spent with Jalal's family in Benghazi, the hospitality they had shown him, he was determined to find his friend's body so that it might be returned to them. After knocking on the doors of countless functionaries in the new revolutionary government, he was finally directed to a Tripoli cemetery where the "traitors"—that is, Qaddafi regime loyalists—had been gathered up and buried.

It was a grim, trash-strewn stretch of land dotted with hundreds of graves. Majdi methodically passed down each row, but Jalal's name wasn't listed. Finally, he came to a far corner of the cemetery where he saw a grave marked "unknown." Majdi felt a burst of excitement, for it occurred to him that given Jalal's terrible head wound, identification might have been impossible—but then he noticed three more graves with the same "unknown" markers. Returning to the cemetery office, he asked for the photographs taken of the unidentified corpses before burial: the faces of all four were so horribly damaged as to be unrecognizable.

Still, Majdi was now convinced that one of the four was Jalal. He broke the news to the Drisi family and several months later flew to Benghazi to pay his respects to them in person. "It was a very emotional meeting," he said, "and I apologized to them for not being able to watch out for Jalal, but . . ." He drifted off in sadness for a moment but then abruptly righted himself, became cheery. "So that is it. Jalal is in one of those four graves, that is for sure. His family has submitted their DNA for testing, and once those results come back, they can identify which one he is and take him back to Benghazi."

Across every culture, it seems almost a primal need for families to recover the physical remains of their lost loved ones, and it was clearly the hope of meeting this need in the Drisi family that had compelled Majdi all those bleak months. But when I gently pointed out to him that DNA identification required a two-way match, which potentially meant the exhumation of all four of the unknown corpses in the Tripoli cemetery—a most unlikely enterprise in postrevolutionary Libya—Majdi stared coolly back at me, a hint of hard challenge in his eyes. Then he gave a thin smile, a quick shrug. "Yes."

But in his quest to learn the fate of his best friend, Majdi had stumbled upon a tragedy of far greater dimension. Every side in the Libyan revolution, it seemed, had taken turns killing off the air force cadets. As in Jalal's case, the Qaddafi forces had used some as bait against the rebels, but they had also executed others for simply trying to go home. In turn, the rebels, after killing many cadets on the battle-field, had executed countless more as "regime loyalists" in the flush of victory. In 2012, scores of cadets who had sur-vived this collective bloodletting were being held in revo-lutionary prisons, while many more were living in hiding.

Wounded Libyan refugee lifted over wall at Tunisian border near Ben Gardane, 2011

Of his approximately 580 colleagues at the Misurata air force academy, Majdi estimates that between 150 and 200 were killed during the war and its immediate aftermath.

"And we were just students," he said. "That's all we were. Both sides used us. Both sides slaughtered us."

Despite all this, Majdi was initially very optimistic about the future in postrevolutionary Libya; the country had oil, smart people, and, after the forty-two-year reign of Muammar el-Qaddafi, the will for a better life. In his view, the first great misstep was when the interim government in Tripoli, the National Transitional Council, announced that it would pay stipends to all those who had fought against the Qaddafi regime. Within weeks, the number of "revolutionaries"— approximately 20,000 by the most generous estimate—had mushroomed to some 250,000. Worse, the structure of the payments, acquiesced to by Western governments allied with the transitional council, created an incentive for new armed groups not just to form but to remain independent of any central command, the better to demand their own share of the compensation pie. Already by the close of 2012, Libyan militias—some composed of true revolutionary veterans, others no more than tribal or criminal gangs—had begun carving the country into rival fiefs, their ability to do so bankrolled by the very central government that they were undermining. That instability was made painfully clear to the Obama administration when the American diplomatic compound in Benghazi was attacked in September 2012, leading to the deaths of Ambassador J. Christopher Stevens and three others. But for Majdi, final disillusionment took a more personal form. In the autumn of 2012, he received his "diploma" from the air force academy, announcing that he had successfully completed all the requirements for a degree in communications engineering.

"I hadn't completed anything," he said. "There had been no classes for a year and a half, so this paper was absolutely meaningless. But this was the new Libya; everything was just lies and corruption. And maybe I felt it more because of what I had gone through, all my friends at the academy who had been killed, but I just couldn't accept that. 'Here, take this paper. No one has to know. Call yourself an engineer.' Maybe others felt it in a different way, or they think of it more in political terms, but it was when I received my diploma that I saw the revolution had been betrayed, that Libya was a failed state."

19

Laila Soueif
Egypt

FOR LAILA SOUEIF, the news of May 28, 2012, couldn't have been worse. That afternoon, Egypt's national election commission announced the names of the two men who would compete in a runoff to become the first democratically elected president in Egyptian history. There had been thirteen candidates, and the only one certain to advance was Mohamed Morsi, the leader of the Muslim Brotherhood, the one party that had unified enough Islamist vot-

ers to form a meaningful voting bloc. Against him, Laila
was ready to support any of the others—save one. That was
Ahmed Shafik, Hosni Mubarak's former prime minister.
That afternoon, it was announced that the runoff contend-
ers were Morsi and Shafik.

"So what to do?" Laila asked rhetorically. "Morsi was
completely unacceptable, but now it was him or Shafik, so
we were stuck. Well, never Shafik—that meant a return to
the Mubarak era—so . . ."

In just this way, Laila Soueif, the stalwart feminist and
liberal, found herself backing the election of a man who
advocated returning Egypt to traditional Islamic values.
Many other Egyptians were aghast at the choice given to
them; in the June runoff, Morsi barely squeaked in with
51.7 percent of the vote.

In his inaugural speech on June 30, Morsi promised that
"in the new Egypt, the president will be an employee, a
servant to the people." But a servant to the deep state may
have been more accurate. Just days before the new president
assumed office, the Supreme Council of the Armed Forces,
or SCAF, the military junta that had ruled Egypt since
Mubarak's overthrow, transferred most presidential powers to the military. That followed a decree by the Supreme
Constitutional Court, a holdover from the Mubarak era,
that dissolved a sitting parliament dominated by the Muslim Brotherhood and other Islamist political parties. On
the day he assumed office, then, Morsi was barely more than
a figurehead, the public face to a democracy already gutted.

But to Laila Soueif, it was a failure foretold. In the parliamentary elections held the previous November, the Mus-

lim Brotherhood and their fellow Islamists had swamped the opposition, taking 69 percent of the seats. Just as Laila had vainly urged the political parties to seize power in Mubarak's last days, so she had spent much of her time since those parliamentary elections imploring the Muslim Brotherhood to do the same.

"Of course I was never a supporter of the Brotherhood," she explained, "but the crucial thing was to take the power out of the hands of SCAF, to move before the whole state apparatus had time to reconsolidate. But the real problem with the Muslim Brotherhood was that they were too moderate for a revolutionary situation. They didn't understand the urgency, and they didn't want to antagonize the state. They thought things would gradually develop, so they ended up doing nothing." Laila shook her head in disgust. "With Mubarak gone, we knew the Brotherhood were the only ones who could change things, because they were the only group that was truly organized. We just didn't know they would handle power so stupidly."

As president, Mohammed Morsi tried mightily to recover the opportunity that had been squandered, and to claw back the authority taken from his office.

Ignoring the fiat of the Supreme Constitutional Court, he ordered the dissolved Islamist-dominated parliament reinstated. Even more boldly, he dismissed the senior military leadership, including the powerful defense minister. In his place, Morsi promoted his own man, Abdel Fattah el-Sisi, the major general who had lectured Laila's husband, Ahmed Seif, during his 2011 detention.

But then Morsi overreached—badly. In October 2012,

he tried to expand the powers of the presidency by decree, a move that alarmed both the deep state and the secular opposition, already growing increasingly fearful of creeping Islamization. Morsi swiftly reeled back some of the more controversial planks in his decree, but the damage was done; in a new round of protests across Egypt, the president was denounced for trying to become a new "pharaoh" or "ayatollah."

And here was the opening the deep state seemed to have been waiting for, the chance to reopen the traditional schism that existed between its Islamist and secular opponents. For decades, the Egyptian generals had held up the Islamists— and most particularly the Muslim Brotherhood—as the greatest threat to the modern secular state and naturally positioned themselves as the guardians against them. This strategy had broken down during the heady days of revolution, with Islamists and progressives alike turning against the generals, but Ahmed Seif had seen how easily it could be resurrected. At a meeting of human rights activists organized by Amnesty International in late 2011, when Egypt was still under the control of the SCAF generals, one attendee after another expressed concern about the possibility of an Islamist electoral victory. As Scott Long—an activist who was at the meeting—recalled on his personal blog, the normally soft-spoken Ahmed finally slapped his hand against the conference table. "I will not accept that the American government, or Amnesty, or anyone, will tell me that I need to tolerate a military dictatorship in order to avoid a takeover by Islamist people," he said. "I will not accept such false choices."

Now, with Morsi's overreach as president, it appeared an increasing number of Egyptians were ready to accept this "false choice."

"It was very clear what the state was doing," Laila said. "First, block everything that Morsi tries to do, so that nothing gets done. 'He's a failed president.' But second, feed the fears about him. That was easy to do, because the propaganda against the Muslim Brotherhood—'They're terrorists'—went back fifty years." It also worked because the propaganda had at least some basis in reality; in the 1990s, several extremist factions of the Muslim Brotherhood had formed alliances with actual terrorist groups.

By the spring of 2013, Egypt was becoming rapidly polarized between Morsi's Muslim Brotherhood followers and nearly everyone else. Perversely, many of the same young demonstrators who took to the streets in 2011 to demand democracy were now calling for Morsi's overthrow. Even more perversely, they looked to the one state institution capable of carrying that out: the Egyptian military.

This wasn't simply a case of national amnesia. One of the more curious aspects of Egyptian society has been a long-standing reverence for its military, a tradition inculcated in Egyptian students from primary school. As a result, even during Mubarak's era, many Egyptians regarded the military as somehow apart from the venal dictatorship and corrupt bureaucracy it upheld. Never mind that the army was, in fact, a prime beneficiary of that corrupt system—the Egyptian military owned construction companies, engineering firms, even a pasta factory—what a lot of those who took to the streets in anti-Morsi demonstrations in 2013 recalled was that the army had been instrumental in finally toppling Mubarak two years before. And if the guardians of the nation had acted to overthrow one dictator, why not a second one in the making?

"You could see what was about to happen," Laila said. "Yes, Morsi was a disaster, he had to go, but to invite in the military was worse. But so many people I knew, even people who had been in Tahrir, this is what they wanted."

On June 30, 2013, the first anniversary of Morsi's inauguration, huge demonstrations took place throughout Egypt, with protesters demanding that he step down. They were met in the streets by counterdemonstrations of Morsi's Muslim Brotherhood supporters. All but invisible between these two great factions was a small group of protesters advocating a third path. It included Laila Soueif and her daughter, Mona.

"We gathered in one corner near Tahrir," Mona recalled with a rueful laugh, "and chanted, 'Not Morsi, and not the army.' People going by gave us these confused looks, like we were all crazy, and I'm sure we kind of seemed that way."

It was at this critical juncture that the defense minister, Abdel Fattah el-Sisi, until then regarded as a bland functionary, finally stepped from the shadows. On July 1, the general delivered an ultimatum to the man who had appointed him, giving Morsi forty-eight hours "to meet the demands of the people" or the army would step in to restore order. Pointing out that he was the elected head of state, the president defiantly dismissed the threat.

"Morsi made two great mistakes," Laila said. "First, he

thought the army wouldn't move against him without the approval of the Americans. He didn't realize the generals didn't care about the Americans anymore. Second, he trusted Sisi."

True to his word, on July 3, Sisi overthrew the Egyptian government—but that was only the beginning. In a sign of what was to come, he also annulled the constitution, arrested Morsi and other Muslim Brotherhood leaders, and shut down four television stations. Within days, he announced the formation of an interim "transitional" government, one composed of military officers and Mubarak-era apparatchiks, but all Egyptians knew that the real authority now lay with Sisi.

It was on the streets of Egypt where the face of the new regime was most nakedly revealed. In the days after Sisi took power, clashes between his supporters and those of the ousted president turned increasingly violent, with the police and the military making very clear whose side they were on. On July 8, security forces fired on Morsi loyalists gathered in central Cairo, killing at least fifty-one. That episode set the stage for far worse. On the afternoon of August 14, security forces moved into Cairo's Rabaa Square with orders to disperse the several thousand Morsi holdout supporters who had been camped there during the previous month. By the most reliable estimates, at least eight hundred and perhaps more than one thousand protesters were killed in the ensuing massacre. In an obscene parody of the 2011 revolution, thousands took to Cairo's streets over the following days to praise the army for its actions in Rabaa.

For Laila Soueif, there was to be another, far more personal indication that the new Egyptian regime was a departure from those that had come before.

Laila's son, Alaa, bore the dubious distinction of having been arrested by all three Egyptian governments that preceded Sisi's takeover: those of Mubarak, SCAF, and Morsi. In 2006, he spent forty-five days in jail for joining a demonstration calling for greater judicial independence. During the SCAF administration, he did a two-month stint in detention for "inciting violence." He had fared better under Morsi, if only because the judges, Mubarak-era holdovers, detested the new president; his March 2013 charge of "inciting aggression" was summarily dismissed, while his conviction for arson resulted in a one-year suspended sentence.

Given this track record, it was probably just a matter of time before Alaa was picked up by the new Egyptian regime. That occurred on November 28, 2013, when he was arrested on charges of inciting violence and, in a nice Orwellian touch, protesting an anti-protest law enacted just four days earlier. That note of black humor aside, under the rule of Sisi, matters were to play out very differently for Laila's son from the way they had in the past.

20

Majd Ibrahim
Syria

ONE OF THE more baffling features of the Syrian Civil War has been the fantastic tangle of tacit cease-fires or temporary alliances that are often forged between various militias and the regime, or even with just a local army commander. These can take any permutation imaginable—radical Islamists teaming up with an Alawite shabiha gang, for example— and they pose a horrifying puzzle to anyone trying to navigate the battlefield, for it means that no one is necessarily who they seem, that death can come from anywhere. But in a curious way, this pattern of secret deal-making also served to long inoculate the Waer district from the scorched-earth tactics the Assad regime was employing elsewhere in Homs since, at any given time, at least some of the myriad rebel militias roaming the neighborhood were apt to be in secret concord with the state.

That dynamic ended in early May 2013. In a colossal misstep, the Free Syrian Army had recently moved back into the devastated Baba Amr neighborhood, and there had been surrounded and slaughtered. Those who managed to escape the regime's cordon made for Waer and took near total control of the enclave. Sure enough, Syrian army artillery shells soon began raining down on Majd's neighborhood. While the scale of shelling was nothing like what had previously befallen Baba Amr or Khalidiya, it was enough to keep the Ibrahim family in their fourth-floor apartment, forever trying to guess where safety lay.

"You just never knew what to do," Majd explained. "Is it better here or in the shelter home? And if it's safer there, how dangerous is it to try to get there?"

As bizarre as it might seem, one reason the Ibrahims stayed on in Homs despite the ever-worsening situation was that Majd's finals were coming up at the university. Their insistence on his finishing was not some homage to the value of higher education, however; under Syrian law, college students were exempt from conscription, so as long as Majd stayed in school, he was safe from being drafted and sent into the military meat grinder. Once he took his exams at the end of July, his parents decided, they would reassess the situation and decide what came next.

That gamble nearly led to disaster. On the afternoon of July 5, Majd was talking with friends on a Waer street when a white station wagon pulled up and three young FSA fighters with Kalashnikovs jumped out. Grabbing Majd, they dragged him into the car where, blindfolded, he was driven to their nearby base.

"I thought it was a joke at the beginning," Majd said. "But they knew my name, my age, what I was studying in the university. They wanted me, not anyone else."

For the next few hours, Majd's captors insisted that

Majd Ibrahim, twenty-four

he admit to being a regime spy, meeting protestations of innocence with kicks and punches. Finally, he was forced to his knees, and an FSA man put a large knife to his throat. Another aimed a Kalashnikov at his head.

"Well, this is the standard way they execute," Majd said softly, "so I knew this was about to happen to me. They wanted to kill me very badly."

In prelude to his execution, however, the chief interrogator thought to look through Majd's cell phone. With each phone number and photograph he flipped to, he demanded that Majd finally give up the identity of his "controller." The twenty-year-old's continued professions of innocence brought more kicks, more punches. The interrogator came to the stored photograph of one young man in particular and stopped.

"Why do you have this guy's photo?" he asked.

"Because he's my best friend," Majd replied.

The FSA commander slowly turned to his captive. "We will call him." The militiaman left the room, and for a long time Majd remained on his knees, the knife to his throat and the gun to his head. Quite unbeknown to Majd, his best friend was also an acquaintance of the FSA commander, and he came to the base to assure the militiaman that Majd Ibrahim was no regime spy. Majd learned this only when the commander returned to the interrogation room and told him he would be set free.

"So that is what saved my life," Majd said, "that photograph."

During the drive back to Waer, the FSA commander delivered a long sales pitch on why Majd should quit the university and take up arms against the regime. The college student said he would think about it.

When Majd arrived at the spot where he had been picked up earlier that day, his parents and friends were waiting for him. The next morning, July 6, the Ibrahim family left for their shelter home, never to return to the Waer neighborhood where Majd had lived his entire life. It was his twenty-first birthday.

Two weeks later, Majd took his exams at the university. With the city increasingly an all-out battlefield, and with his nearly fatal encounter with the FSA fresh in their memory, Majd's parents decided that all three Ibrahim children should go to Damascus, along with their mother; Majd's father was determined to remain in Homs.

"At that point, we had lost almost everything," Majd recalled. "We had sold our car and most of our furniture, but I think for my father it was psychologically important to stay, to try to protect what little we had left."

In Damascus, the veneer of normality continued, even if it had begun to fray a bit as the civil war entered its third year. While couples continued to stroll in downtown and the central bazaar remained a busy place, there frequently came the sound of distant rumbling, much like thunder, as battles raged in the suburbs.

Majd was still in Damascus in late August 2013 when he heard rumors of an enormous battle in the rebel-held neighborhood of Ghouta, with many hundreds dead. As details slowly emerged over the following days, Majd learned the August 21 death toll in Ghouta was not the result of battle but rather of a chemical weapons attack, reportedly carried out by the Syrian army.

Precisely one year before, President Obama had warned the Assad regime of the grave repercussions it would face if it ever employed chemical weapons in the war. Obama had underscored that warning as recently as March 2013, reiterating the "red line" that would be crossed by such an attack, and how it would be a "game changer" as far as the United States' nonintervention policy in Syria. Within days of the Ghouta attack, a United Nations inspection team determined that the estimated 1,400 dead had been killed with shells of sarin gas, taken from known Syrian government stockpiles and "most likely" fired from government lines.

"When we heard that," Majd said, "we all expected a big reaction, that the Americans would now come in." Curiously, that expectation wasn't shared by the Syrian military units deployed around Damascus, all of whom appeared unusually relaxed. "It was very strange, but it was like they knew nothing was going to happen."

They were right. Although President Obama had the executive prerogative to order retaliatory air strikes, he balked in the face of fierce opposition by both Democrats and Republicans in Congress, then sidestepped the matter by requesting congressional authorization before taking any action. In a particularly humiliating gesture, Secretary of State John Kerry was dispatched to Capitol Hill to promise that any punitive military action against the Assad regime would be extremely limited, which rather begged the question of why it was being contemplated at all.

In the end, Russia, an Assad ally, saved the Obama administration further embarrassment by offering to oversee the removal of Syria's chemical weapons stockpiles. If some in the American administration saw this as a face-saving compromise, this was not at all the way it was viewed in the Middle East. There, it served to confirm that American "red lines" were meaningless, a point that emboldened America's enemies and infuriated and frightened its friends. In light of what was to come, it may well have been the most grievous American policy misstep in the region since the Iraqi invasion.

21

Khulood al-Zaidi
Jordan

SINCE HER RETURN from San Francisco in 2009, Khulood had been marooned in Jordan. By 2014, she was living in a small apartment in a working-class neighborhood of eastern Amman with her father and two sisters, Teamim and Sahar. It was a dreary place, a three-story walk-up overlooking a dusty commercial road, but it was softened by the presence of Mystery, the sisters' pet cat, and Shiny, a small box turtle they had rescued from the street.

Before leaving for the United States in 2008, Khulood had briefly worked for a Japanese humanitarian organization called Kokkyo naki Kodomotachi (Children Without Borders), or KnK, and she rejoined the agency upon her return to Amman the following year. Her principal task was to help acclimate some of the countless thousands of Iraqi children whose families had fled to Jordan to escape the war, and so impressed were the KnK supervisors with Khulood's connection to the children that they soon hired her two sisters as well. Around the same time, Ali al-Zaidi, the retired radiologist and patriarch of the family, found

A young Iraqi refugee with her brother in Damascus, Syria, February 2008

work on the loading docks of a yogurt factory on the indus-
trial outskirts of Amman. In 2014, the family was at least
scraping by.

Khulood's work at KnK had undergone a shift, though.
With the war in Iraq having abated, the number of Iraqi
refugees in Jordan was dramatically reduced from its half-
million peak. They were soon replaced, however, by new
refugees from the war in Syria—just a trickle at first, but
by the end of 2014, their number was more than six hundred thousand.

In certain ways, Khulood found the Syrian children quite
different from their Iraqi counterparts. "The Iraqis, because
they had become so tired of war, they were very peaceful and
easy to work with. But the Syrian children—the boys—
they have this idea, 'We have to go back to Syria to fight.'
They hear this constantly from their fathers—'You're going

to be a soldier and go back to Syria'—so they're like little rebels, not little kids. It's all about home, missing home, how they need to go back and avenge what happened." By contrast, the girls of the two countries had far more in common. "In both Iraq and Syria, girls are taught to keep everything inside. They aren't listened to. This makes it much harder to reach them, so their problems are deeper."

Khulood still hadn't given up on her quest to get her family out of the region. For several years, she had continued to petition for the United States to reopen their case, but those efforts went nowhere. By 2014, she was holding out special hope for Britain; at one time, she had worked as an interpreter for a British film company in Jordan, and with letters of support from her former coworkers, Khulood reasoned, the authorities there might look favorably on her. She had recently become aware of a rather diabolical catch-22, however. Nearly the only way to win asylum in Britain—or in any other country, for that matter—was to present the petition in person. To do that, Khulood first needed to obtain a British visa, and to get that, she needed to have legal residency in Jordan. "And that's impossible," she said. "Jordan only gives residency to wealthy refugees who, of course, have no problem resettling in Europe anyway."

Still, in April 2014, Khulood hadn't completely lost hope. Possessed of a seemingly unconquerable will, over several days of conversation, she was determined to put the very best face on her situation and was far more interested in talking up her current escape plans than her past failures. Only once did this brave facade crack, and it came amid a discussion about the future she imagined for the refugee children she worked with.

"I stay with this because I want these kids to have a better life than me," she said, "but frankly, I think their lives will be wasted just like mine. I try not to think that way, but, really, let's be candid: this is their future. For me, these past nine years have been wasted. My sisters and I, we have dreams. We are educated, we want to study, to have careers. But in Jordan, we cannot legally work, and we cannot leave, so we are just standing in place. That's all. Now we're becoming old, we're all in our thirties, but still we can't marry or start families, because then we will never get out of here."

Khulood sat back and let out a dispirited sigh. "I'm sorry. I try to never pity myself or to blame anyone for this situation, but I really wish the Americans had thought more about what they were doing before they came to Iraq. That's what started all this. Without that, we would be normal."

But for Khulood and her sisters, the situation was about to grow even worse. In the autumn of 2014, Khulood said, KnK was having problems with the Jordanian government, which insisted that the organization's foreign staff members have legal work permits—permits the al-Zaidi sisters didn't possess. While KnK said the sisters' work was exemplary, its efforts to keep them were in vain; that December, all three Zaidi sisters were dismissed from their jobs on the same day.

22

Laila Soueif
Egypt

ON OCTOBER 27, 2014, Laila Soueif and her oldest daughter, Mona, climbed the short row of steps leading to the main entrance of the Egyptian supreme court building, then stopped and sat beside one of its stone columns. From her backpack, Laila drew out a small sign written on cardboard. It announced she and her daughter were going to intensify the partial hunger strike they had begun in September to protest the injustices committed against their family. They would remain there off and on for the next forty-eight hours, taking no food or liquids.

"The idea wasn't to kill ourselves," Laila explained, "but to draw attention to what the Sisi regime was doing. It was the only weapon we had left." As for its efficacy, she was matter-of-fact. "A few people passing signaled that they supported us—sometimes quite a subtle signal."

Adding another layer of pain to the experience, it came at a time when Laila's family was, quite literally, disappearing before her eyes.

The first sign that the Sisi regime was to take a much

dimmer view than its predecessors of dissent to its rule came with Alaa's arrest in late November 2013. Rather than being released on bail to await trial, he and his twenty-four codefendants were held for the next four months. In a tactic apparently designed to break his will, Alaa's release on bail in March 2014 had been followed by his rearrest three months later.

If average Egyptians were alarmed by the deepening repression in their country—less than a year after Sisi took power, there were already far more political prisoners in Egypt's jails than there had ever been under Mubarak— they gave scant evidence of it. In presidential elections that May, Sisi, now officially retired from the military, won with more than 96 percent of the vote. While this surely wasn't a wholly accurate reflection of his popularity—between those political parties that had been banned and those that boycotted the election, Sisi faced only token opposition—even an ardent opponent like Laila Soueif recognized that the former general enjoyed widespread support. She had even seen it among many of her friends and university coworkers. "They had this idea that, 'Okay, maybe he's a little rough, but he saved us from the Islamists,'" she said. "That's all they cared about, all they saw."

Until then, Laila's youngest daughter, the twenty-two-year-old Sanaa, had avoided the family tradition of run-ins with the law. On June 21, 2014, that changed. Increasingly infuriated by the treatment of her brother and Egypt's other political prisoners, Sanaa joined a human rights rally in Cairo. Within minutes, she was arrested on precisely the same charge as her brother: violating the protest law.

Even under the tightening Sisi regime, members of the Cairene upper class like Sanaa enjoyed a degree of immunity—the main enemies of the state, after all, were the working-class followers of the Muslim Brotherhood, and they were to be ruthlessly hunted down—but when brought before a magistrate, the college student took a bold step. Despite suggestions from the judge that she stay quiet, Sanaa insisted that she had been a chief organizer of the rally and refused to sign her statement until this detail was included. "She wasn't going to let them do the usual thing of letting the high-profile activists go and pound on the lesser-known ones," Laila said. For this principled stand, Sanaa, like her older brother, was held in jail pending trial.

For Ahmed Seif, Egypt's preeminent human rights lawyer, it had meant that his ever-expanding roster of clients now included two of his own children. At a news conference the previous January, the former political prisoner took the microphone to eloquently address his imprisoned son, Alaa. "I wanted you to inherit a democratic society that guards your rights, my son, but instead I passed on the prison cell that held me, and now holds you." By June, that haunting message applied equally to his youngest daughter.

Soon, matters turned even darker for the family of Laila Soueif. Long in frail health, Ahmed had been scheduled for open-heart surgery at the end of August; on the sixteenth of that month, he suddenly collapsed and then fell into a coma. Only after intense lobbying by both influential Egyptians and international human rights organizations did the Sisi regime grant Alaa and Sanaa afternoon furloughs to visit their father before he died.

"And that was the absolute worst day," Laila said, "maybe the worst day of my life. Sanaa was being held in a police station, so we had been able to see her and tell her what was going on, but Alaa had no idea. He showed up at the hospital with flowers for Ahmed, so I had to take him aside to say his father was in a coma. He said, 'So he won't even know I'm here, then,' and just threw the flowers out."

The day after that hospital visit, Alaa went on a hunger strike in his cell. On August 28, the day of her father's funeral, Sanaa stopped eating also. A week later, Laila and Mona announced their partial hunger strike.

In light of both Ahmed's death and the family's prominence, many observers believed that Alaa and Sanaa would be shown leniency by the courts. That belief was misplaced. On October 26, 2014, Sanaa was sentenced to three years in prison for violating the protest law. The next day, Laila and Mona took to the courthouse steps for their intensified hunger strike. Laila braced herself for more bad news when Alaa went to trial the following month, by remembering something her husband had said.

"Because Ahmed had spent so much time in courtrooms and knew what certain things meant," she said, "he was always very accurate in his predictions. Before he died, when he was still representing Alaa, he told me, 'Prepare yourself, because they're going to give him five years.'"

23

Majd Ibrahim
Syria

BY THE TIME Laila had begun her hunger strike and Khulood and her sisters were losing their jobs, Majd Ibrahim had himself found a moment of respite—one that, although brief, had been a long time coming.

In late 2013, the Ibrahim family had returned to Homs from Damascus, only to discover that, with the serial siege steadily grinding ever more of the city's neighborhoods to dust, even their shelter home was no longer safe. In March 2014, the family had moved once again, this time to New Akrama, a neighborhood near downtown that had been spared the worst of the violence. There, they simply waited along with everyone else for something, anything, to change.

That change finally came in May, when the last of Homs's rebels accepted a brokered cease-fire and safe passage from the city. The three-year siege of Homs was over. What had once been a vibrant, cosmopolitan city was now known as Syria's Stalingrad, with vast expanses of its neighborhoods uninhabitable. It was also only then that the full horror of what many of its residents had been subjected to came to light. In the total-war environment, some trapped residents had starved to death, while others had survived by eating leaves and weeds.

But even if a kind of peace had reached the shattered streets of Homs, the war continued elsewhere in Syria, and in a form that boded poorly for all its citizens. Majd Ibrahim heard the names of so many new militias competing with the plethora of already existing ones that it was quite impossible to keep track of them all. For sheer daring and cruelty, however, one group stood out: the Islamic State, or ISIS.

Comprising an even more radical offshoot of Al Qaeda, the newcomers attracted Islamic extremists from around the world. In Syria, the group announced its presence with a series of sudden, brutal attacks in Aleppo and the desert towns to the east, battling not just the Syrian army but any rival militias it deemed "apostate." What most drew the attention of Majd Ibrahim was the group's reputation for complete mercilessness, for eliminating by the most horrific means possible any who would resist its will.

Just a month after the Homs siege ended, most of the rest of the world would hear of ISIS, too, when it stormed out of the Syrian desert to utterly transform the Middle Eastern battlefield yet again.

PART IV

ISIS Rising

2014–2015

24

Wakaz Hassan
Iraq

WAKAZ HASSAN SPEAKS in a loud, slightly atonal voice, and in conversation often asks for things to be repeated. From this, it seems possible he suffers from an undiagnosed hearing impairment, which might also help explain the difficulties he always had in school. "I was unable to memorize the curriculum," he said. "I felt whenever I tried to study, I failed."

After being forced to repeat a year of school, Wakaz simply dropped out.

By the time he was a teenager, he had joined the legions of other unskilled young Iraqi men who, while living in the family home, scraped by with day-labor construction jobs: hauling bricks, cutting rebar, mixing cement. When no construction work was to be had, Wakaz sometimes helped out in the small candy shop that his father, a retired bank clerk, had opened in Dawr, his home village just outside Tikrit, but it was all a rather meager and dull existence.

There was one potential way out. In stark contrast to Wakaz's own middling ability to find employment, his oldest brother, twenty-six-year-old Mohammed, had been hired as an intelligence officer for the local security forces, and this sinecure held out considerable promise for the entire Hassan family. Given the culture of nepotism that Saddam Hussein had fostered in Iraq, and which continued to flourish after his demise, Wakaz could reasonably hope that Mohammed might someday work his way far enough up into the municipal ranks to bring his three younger brothers, including himself, into the security forces as well. But in June 2014, a series of cataclysmic events was about to break over the Sunni heartland of Iraq, and they would radically alter the fortunes of the nineteen-year-old day laborer in Dawr.

At the very beginning of that year, ISIS insurgents had wrested control of the crucial crossroads city of Fallujah in Iraq's Anbar Province, then spread out to seize a number of nearby cities and towns. At the time, Wakaz knew very little about the group, other than that it sought to establish an Islamic caliphate in the Sunni lands of Iraq and Syria. Over subsequent months, however, Wakaz, like most other young Tikriti men, had seen the elaborate recruitment videos that ISIS produced and distributed on social media. These videos depicted warriors, or "knights," as ISIS called them, clad in smartly turned-out uniforms and black ski masks as they rode triumphantly through towns they had conquered, great black flags flapping from their new Toyota Land Cruisers. Other videos from that time showed a decidedly darker side of ISIS—executions and crucifixion displays—but Wakaz claimed never to have seen those. In any event, the budding caliphate seemed far away from the sleepy and economically moribund town of Dawr.

By that June, it was far away no more. On June 6, a band of ISIS fighters entered the western suburbs of Mosul, northern Iraq's largest city, just 140 miles up Highway 1 from Tikrit. Although it's estimated that a mere 1,500 ISIS fighters participated in the attack on Mosul—and by some accounts, the number was far lower—within a couple of days, they had put the tens of thousands of Iraqi army and security forces in the city of two million to panicked flight. By June 9, the Highway 1 bypass road around Tikrit was the scene of a frantic stampede as thousands of Iraqi soldiers, many having already shed their uniforms, sped for the safety of Baghdad, one hundred miles farther south. But ISIS wasn't done. After Mosul, they quickly advanced on Baiji, the oil-refinery town forty miles north of Tikrit, and then on June 11 rolled into Tikrit itself.

In Tikrit, just as in Mosul and Baiji, the Iraqi army offered virtually nothing in the way of resistance, with different units seeming only to compete on how quickly they could escape and how much of their weaponry they could leave behind for the enemy. But if the army fled the region, few of the local people did. Those remaining behind included Wakaz and his brother Mohammed.

The ISIS offensive of June 2014 marked one of the most stunning military feats in modern history. In less than one week, a lightly armed guerrilla force of as few as five thousand fighters scattered a modern and well-equipped army at least twenty times its size, capturing billions of dollars' worth of advanced weaponry and military hardware, and now controlled population centers that totaled some five million people. While such a colossal collapse as that experienced by the Iraqi army must necessarily be a result of many failures—certainly, incompetence and corruption played major roles—much of it could be attributed to recent history.

Under the eight-year rule of Prime Minister Nouri Kamal al-Maliki, Iraq's Shiite majority had come to dominate most every aspect of the national government, including its military, and to lord their newfound primacy over the Sunnis. For many residents in the Sunni heartland—and this included Baiji and Tikrit—this heavy-handed treatment spawned a deep contempt for both the central government and its army, whom they regarded as occupiers. Of course, that Shiite-dominated army was well aware of the locals' contempt and deeply distrusted them in turn, to such an extent that at the first sign of trouble—in this case, a few Sunni jihadists riding into town vowing vengeance— the soldiers, fearing a mass uprising against them, simply bolted.

But this was not a completely unfounded fear, because what ISIS had very cleverly done was to establish sleeper cells in these cities ahead of time, both to initiate attacks when the battle was joined and to recruit new members to the cause. Among those recruits in the town of Dawr was Wakaz Hassan.

According to Wakaz, he joined ISIS on June 10, 2014, just as the guerrilla group became active in the Tikrit area but a full day before its attacks there began in earnest. His chief recruiter, he claimed, was none other than his brother, the twenty-six-year-old American-trained and Iraqi government—employed intelligence officer Moham-med. "It wasn't for religion," Wakaz maintained, "and it wasn't as if I had any emotional connection to the group—at that point, I didn't really know what they were fighting for—but because Mohammed said we should join."

Omitted from Wakaz's account was the matter of money. By the summer of 2014, ISIS was so flush with funds from its control of the oil fields of eastern Syria that it could offer even untrained foot soldiers up to $400 a month for enlisting—vastly more than an unskilled nineteen-year-old like Wakaz could make from pickup construction jobs. Of course, having now also seized the Baiji oil refinery, ISIS stood to turn its financial spigot into a geyser.

As pledging members of ISIS, Mohammed and Wakaz assisted in the seizing of Tikrit on June 11. The brothers also played at least a supporting role in the most horrific atrocity to occur during ISIS's atrocity-laden June blitzkrieg.

Just to the north of Tikrit is a large Iraqi military train-ing base still known by its American name: Camp Speicher. Thousands of cadets were undergoing training there when ISIS closed in. As might have been predicted from the con-duct of Iraqi soldiers elsewhere, the regular army units and senior military command garrisoned at Speicher simply fled the compound at word of ISIS's approach, leaving the students stranded. Wakaz was among those ISIS members who helped round up the cadets on June 12, but insists he played no role in what came next.

After separating the trainees by sect—Sunni to one side,

Shiite to the other—ISIS gunmen marched hundreds of the Shiite cadets to various spots around Tikrit to be machine-gunned, the mass murders dutifully videotaped by ISIS cameramen for posting on the Internet. Traditionally, armies and guerrilla groups try to deny or minimize their war crimes, but not so with ISIS; when outside observers first estimated that 800 cadets were murdered that day in Tikrit, ISIS spokesmen boasted that they had actually killed many more. (The final death toll remains unknown, but estimates now range as high as 1,700.)

After the Camp Speicher massacre, Wakaz signed up with ISIS for a one-year enlistment—for a terrorist organization, it has a surprisingly formal bureaucracy—and was ferried up Highway 1 with a large group of fellow recruits to an ISIS compound outside Mosul. There, he learned the rudimentary skills imparted to new soldiers everywhere: running obstacle courses, breaking down and firing various weapons, tactical drills on maintaining squad cohesion on the battlefield. But soon enough his training took a more brutal turn.

On a morning in late June, Wakaz was summoned from his barracks by a senior commander. Instructing the teenager to follow, the commander led Wakaz to a field at the edge of the compound. After a few moments, they were joined by two other men, an ISIS fighter and a civilian who appeared to be in his thirties. The civilian was blindfolded, with his hands tied behind his back, and he was crying. The ISIS fighter roughly forced the crying man to his knees as the commander handed Wakaz a pistol. The former day laborer from Dawr knew precisely what was expected of him.

Wakaz Hassan demonstrating how his
ISIS trainer taught him to perform an
execution, December 2015

"They showed me how to do it," Wakaz said. "You point
the gun downward. Also to not shoot directly at the center
of the head, but to go a little bit off to one side."

In the training-compound field, Wakaz dutifully carried
out his first execution. Over the following few weeks, he
was summoned to the field five more times, to murder five
more blindfolded and handcuffed men. "I didn't know anything about them," he said, "but I would say they ranged in
age from about thirty-five to maybe seventy. After that first
one, only one other was crying. With the others, I think
maybe they didn't know what was about to happen."

Wakaz related all this—even physically acted out how
a proper killing was done—with no visible emotion. But
then, as if belatedly realizing the cold-bloodedness of his
account, he gave a small shrug.

"I felt bad doing it," he said, "but I had no choice. Once we reached Mosul, there was no way to leave—and with ISIS, if you don't obey, they kill you too."

25

Azar Mirkhan
Kurdistan

DURING OUR WELL-ARMED drive to northern Iraq in May 2015, Dr. Azar Mirkhan spoke of his father, the man who had helped lead the 1974 Kurdish uprising against the Iraq government and who had then taken his family across the mountains into exile in Iran. Due to Heso Mirkhan's prominence in the Peshmerga—and Iranian nervousness about their own Kurdish population—the family had initially been forced to live in a Kurd-free city in central Iran, a stricture that was lifted when the Iran-Iraq War started in 1980 and the Khomeini regime suddenly saw a use for the Iraqi Kurd exiles in their midst. Moving his burgeoning family—it would ultimately grow to ten sons and four daughters—to Iranian Kurdistan, Mirkhan resumed his Peshmerga leadership role, as well as his cross-border incursions. That caught up with him in April 1983, when he was killed in an ambush in northern Iraq.

"I don't really remember him that well, because I was only eight when he died," Azar said. "My strongest memory is that there was just a constant parade of Peshmerga commanders coming to our house, conferring with my father."

For nearly thirty years, Heso's remains were lost somewhere in the mountains of Kurdistan, but a few years ago, Azar and his brothers began a months-long quest to locate them. By talking with villagers and Heso's surviving companions, they finally found his bones at the bottom of a remote ravine.

"We brought them back to our village, and he was given a hero's funeral," Azar said. "Even Barzani was there"—the KRG's president, Massoud Barzani.

The doctor's sense of personal loss was more evident when he talked of the death of his brother Ali, the second oldest of the fourteen Mirkhan siblings and the first to follow Heso into the ranks of Peshmerga leadership. "When Ali was killed, it was a tragedy not just for the family but all Kurdistan," Azar said. "He was a natural leader of men— charismatic, brilliant—and, okay, he was my brother, but I believe we would be in a very different place now if he had stayed alive. Many, many people who knew him have said this to me."

Azar told me those stories perhaps in part to explain why our destination that day, a little village in Iraq called Gunde Siba, still haunted him. He was on an indefinite leave of absence from the hospital where he worked in Erbil, the KRG capital, to devote all his energies to confronting the crisis caused by the ISIS invasion of the previous year. His duties, which appeared to be largely self-determined, consisted of periodically touring the Peshmerga front lines and advising its commanders. Everyone in the KRG, it seemed, knew the Mirkhan name, and one of its happier consequences was that its bearers could expect to be treated with immediate respect and deference.

As we spoke, it became clear that Azar's self-appointed mission went far beyond confronting the threat of ISIS. He saw in the KRG's current situation a precious and unprecedented opportunity to create a true Kurdish nation. To achieve that meant not just defeating the ISIS fanatics but ridding the land of the Kurds' historical enemies, the Arabs, once and for all. "For fourteen hundred years, they have sworn to destroy us," he said. "At what point do we take them at their word?" To Azar, that point had now been reached. In his view, which is by no means a minority one in the KRG, the first task at hand is to sever the remaining vestiges of the Iraqi state—it is a point of pride with Azar that he doesn't speak Arabic and has only once been to Baghdad—and then to dismantle the legacy of forced Arab-Kurd integration initiated by Saddam Hussein.

But time was running out. At about the midpoint on our drive, we were passing an unassuming farming village when Azar slowed the car to a crawl, gave a disdainful click of his teeth. To me, the village was indistinguishable from a hundred others we'd passed, but Azar saw something quite different.

"This is our problem right here. Forty years ago, this village was all Kurdish, except for maybe one or two Arab families. But now the Arabs have almost completely taken over because they breed like rabbits. That's why I always tell Kurds, 'Never sell your land to Arabs. No matter how poor you are, never sell to them.' It should be a law."

Part of the doctor's severity stems from what he regards as Kurdish complacency in the face of the dangers that lay all around, and it is further fueled by the tragedy he witnessed in Gunde Siba on August 3, 2014.

For twenty-two years after its creation in 1992, the KRG was a relative oasis of stability and peace in the region, its ties to Baghdad ever more theoretical. That exempt status was most nakedly revealed during the American intervention in Iraq, in which the KRG openly sided with the invaders, providing them with back bases and airfields from which to carry out the fight; as local officials are fond of pointing out, not a single coalition soldier was killed in the KRG during the Iraq War. That calm continued through the steady disintegration of Iraq after the American withdrawal, as the KRG became ever more reluctant to pay even lip service to affiliation with Baghdad. To the good citizens of the KRG, it increasingly appeared that their mountain enclave had somehow found a way to escape the maelstroms swirling around it, that the days of warrior families like the Mirkhans might go the way of folklore. That fanciful notion ended with ISIS's lightning advance into central Iraq in June 2014.

"I've never trusted the Arabs, but as strange as it sounds, I trusted Daesh," Azar explained, using a common, vaguely pejorative term for ISIS. "In the past, the Arabs always lied—'Oh, you Kurds have nothing to fear from us'—and

Azar Mirkhan, forty-one, inspecting an ISIS execution site outside Sinjar, 2015

then they attacked us. But Daesh was absolutely clear what they were going to do. They wanted to take this part of the world back to the caliphate. They wanted to eliminate everyone who was not their kind—the Christians and the Kurds and the Shia—and they were absolutely open about it. After their June offensive, I had no doubt they were coming for us next." The doctor even pinpointed where they would strike first. "Any fool looking at a map could know. It was going to be the Yazidis. It was going to be Sinjar."

The Yazidis are a Kurdish religious minority that ISIS had long excoriated as "devil worshipers" and vowed to exterminate. Making them especially vulnerable, their Mount Sinjar homeland was in the far northwestern corner of Iraq and outside official KRG territory. What's more—and this is what a glance at a map made obvious—with ISIS's capture of Mosul that June, the land link between the KRG and the Yazidi Kurds in Sinjar was reduced to a single rutted farm road.

In the days and weeks after the June offensive, Azar made use of his family name to compel meetings within his circle of civilian and military comrades. At each, he warned of the coming ISIS attack. "No one took it seriously," he recalled. "They all said, 'No, their fight is with the Shia in Baghdad. Why would they come here?' They just didn't see what was about to happen."

On August 1, 2014, ISIS guerrillas attacked an isolated Peshmerga outpost in the town of Zumar, which lay just ten miles away from the last road into Sinjar. When still there was no sign of action by the Kurdish government, in desperation, Azar Mirkhan rustled up five or six of his Peshmerga friends, and together they raced west.

"And this is as far as we got," Azar said. "Right here."

We were standing on the shoulder of the road in Gunde Siba, just a few miles west of the Tigris River and still some forty miles from the town of Sinjar. "By then, it was night, and right here we started meeting the Peshmerga who had fled from Sinjar and, behind them, the Yazidi refugees. It was impossible to go on because the road was just jammed, everyone trying to escape. We set up a defense post here and rallied some of the Peshmerga to stay with us, but this is as far as we got." He lit a cigarette and blew smoke into the air. "We were one day too late."

In Sinjar that day—August 3—ISIS began carrying out

mass executions, a slaughter that would ultimately claim the lives of at least five thousand Yazidis.

They were also rounding up thousands of girls and women to be used as sex slaves. Tens of thousands more Yazidis were frantically scaling the flanks of Mount Sinjar in a bid to escape the killers. Of all this, Azar Mirkhan had only an intimation in the terror-stricken faces and anguished accounts of those survivors streaming into Gunde Siba.

But Azar had little time to grasp, let alone address, the tragedy unfolding in Sinjar. Just two days later, ISIS began a second offensive, this one aimed directly at the KRG capital city of Erbil. Turning back from Gunde Siba, the doctor raced south for the battlefield.

26

Majd Ibrahim
Syria

FOR MOST OF 2014, the Ibrahim family lived in comparative safety in their new home in central Homs. With a citywide cease-fire forged that May, most new fighting had moved to the far suburbs. As improbable as it might seem, the cease-fire also led to the reopening of the Safir Hotel, where Majd's father worked; beginning that September, Majd took a job serving as the Safir's receptionist. "With the cease-fire, everything was better," Majd recalled. "I wouldn't say back to normal, because so much of the city was destroyed by then, but you could see that life was coming back."

The sense of growing calm was shattered on the morning of October 1, 2014. Majd was at work at the Safir when he received a frantic phone call from his mother. There had just been an explosion at Akrama al-Makhzomeh, the school attended by Majd's eleven-year-old younger brother, Ali, with reports of many casualties.

His mother raced to the scene, but Majd was unable to leave work for another ninety minutes. The memory of what he saw when he finally arrived at the school cast the perennially cheerful Majd into a dark corner within himself, his eyes settling into a sad, distant stare.

"Never could I have imagined something like that," he said. "It was like a nightmare, the worst nightmare. Blood everywhere, parts of children, and they're everywhere around you, and you're walking through all this—you're stepping on body parts . . ." He closed his eyes briefly, struggled to control his breathing. "It's something I can just never get out of my mind."

It was only when Majd learned the details of what had happened, though, that he grasped the full savagery of the attack. Just as parents and rescuers began swarming into Akrama al-Makhzomeh in response to the first blast, from a car bomb, a suicide bomber tried to enter the school's main courtyard to kill more; shut out by an alert guard, the bomber blew himself up at the front gate. When Majd's mother reached the bomb site, she found Ali hiding with a group of terrified classmates at the back of the school.

The double bombing at Akrama al-Makhzomeh killed at

least forty-five, including forty-one schoolchildren. It was another reminder—as if the people of Homs needed one—that in the new Syria, no haven was truly safe, no place off limits to the murderers. In its aftermath, the Ibrahim family, like almost everyone else in the New Akrama neighborhood, largely stayed indoors, venturing outside only when necessary.

27

Wakaz Hassan
Iraq

AFTER COMPLETING HIS three months of basic training at the ISIS camp in Mosul, Wakaz Hassan was sent back to his hometown of Dawr. There, he said, his main duty consisted of manning ISIS checkpoints. In early 2015, he was redeployed to the oil town of Baiji, where a joint Iraqi army and Shiite militia force was attempting to wrest back control of the refineries. In Wakaz's telling, his main posting in Baiji was in a second-line defensive position, watching over one sector of the vast oil-refinery complex for any sign of enemy encroachment. The experience left him unimpressed with the fighting prowess of the Iraqi army.

"The Shia [militias] were braver because they hated us and wanted to take revenge," he explained, "but the [regular] soldiers were bad. A lot of them, the Sunnis, were coming over to surrender to us."

It was in Baiji that Wakaz first came into contact with some of the foreign fighters who had flocked to the region in answer to ISIS's call. Many of the Syrian and Iraqi fighters deeply resented the foreigners—they received better housing and better food, and were often the first in line to be given "wives," or sex slaves, once the ISIS leadership had taken their pick—but Wakaz didn't share that sentiment. "Most of them were very religious and had truly studied the Koran," he said, "and they had come there to be *shaheeds* [martyrs]. They were waiting to be called [to carry out suicide attacks], so I think it was right that they had more to enjoy than the others."

Wakaz couldn't directly communicate with most of the foreign fighters—the majority in Baiji, he recalled, were from the Muslim republics of the former Soviet Union and didn't speak Arabic—but he felt a kinship with them for their devout religious beliefs. "I didn't know the Koran very well, but to see men willing to die for it, it showed me the power it has."

When I asked if he ever considered becoming a *shaheed*, Wakaz shook his head, but then shrugged. "Anyway, it wouldn't have happened. I'm not educated, I don't know the Koran, so they would not have selected me."

28

Azar Mirkhan
Kurdistan

"I LIKE FIGHTING DAESH," Azar said. "They're actually quite smart. It's almost a kind of game."

It was May 2015, and we were at a forward Peshmerga firebase about forty miles southwest of Erbil, in an area known as the Gwer-Makhmour front. The firebase consisted of a series of hastily constructed berms and dugouts on a ridgeline about three miles from the Tigris River, with ISIS in control of the lowlands below. Azar had survived several ISIS attacks along this stretch of the front.

"First, they send in their suicide bombers in armored Humvees. If you don't destroy them as they come up the hill—and you need to make a direct hit—they'll blast huge holes in the walls, because these are just massive explosions. Then in the confusion of that, they send in their infantry and, behind them, the snipers. It all happens very fast: everything quiet, and then suddenly they're everywhere. The important thing is to stay calm, to pick your targets, because if you panic, you're finished. That's the problem with the Iraqi army; they always panic."

Panic didn't seem to figure prominently in Azar's range of emotions. Leading the way up to the firebase parapet, he propped his elbows on the sandbags to train his binoculars on an ISIS-held village, perhaps seven hundred or eight hundred yards away down the hillside. All was very still there, save for two of the distinctive ISIS black-and-white flags curling in the light breeze.

A soldier below the parapet called out a warning: an ISIS sniper had been spotted in the village an hour earlier, and, in his current stance, Azar made for a very easy target. The doctor gave the soldier an irritated look, then turned back to his binoculars.

It was along this front in early August 2014 that ISIS had launched their offensive in a bid to capture Erbil, the KRG capital, and it was the same battlefield that Azar had raced for after his failed attempt to reach Sinjar.

As it happened, Azar's older brother Araz, forty-four, was the deputy commander of Peshmerga forces along that portion of the KRG frontier, Sector 6, and Azar immediately went into battle alongside his brother—but not just Araz. Most of Azar's other brothers had long since moved abroad as part of the Kurdish diaspora and had become doctors and engineers in the United States and Europe, but befitting the Mirkhan family's warrior-caste reputation, most of them set aside their businesses and medical practices to race to the KRG and take up arms. At one point in that summer, five Mirkhan brothers, along with one of Azar's nephews, were fighting shoulder to shoulder at a Sector 6 firebase.

"It was a good thing ISIS didn't drop a mortar on us right then," Azar joked. "Our mother would have been upset."

Azar Mirkhan on the front line in Sinjar, June 2015

But something did happen in the battle that changed Azar. After coming within fifteen miles of Erbil, the ISIS advance stalled and was then thrown back by a furious Peshmerga counteroffensive. During that counterattack on August 20, an ISIS sniper's bullet shattered Azar's right hand. For weeks afterward, there was concern that he might lose the hand altogether, but surgery and physical therapy helped restore some function. Still, in May 2015, nine months after the shooting, the doctor could only shake hands with his left, and spent hours each day gently curling and uncurling the fingers of his right.

"The important thing is that I can shoot a gun again now," Azar said. "Not as well as before, but almost."

Perhaps not surprising in a people so implacably committed to establishing a homeland, the Kurds of the KRG find it intolerable that ISIS should maintain dominion over any of their territory. Much as the United States Army will sustain more casualties in order to retrieve their battlefield dead, so the Peshmerga have been willing to suffer higher losses to recover Kurdish ground more quickly.

At Black Tiger Camp, the back-base command center of Sector 6, Sirwan Barzani, the overall sector commander, could point to the enormous color-coded battlefront map on his office wall and rattle off statistics remarkable in their specificity. "When I first arrived here," he said, "Daesh was just three kilometers down the road. Now we have cleared them for twenty-three kilometers to the west and thirty-four kilometers to the south. In my sector, we have retaken eleven hundred square kilometers, but we still have about two hundred fourteen square kilometers to go."

By May 2015, Barzani said, nearly 120 Peshmerga had died in Sector 6, where the greatest ISIS incursions had occurred. At the same time, Kurdish commanders make an interesting distinction between where they are willing to suffer losses to regain land and where they aren't. For example, the ISIS-held village that Azar had studied with his binoculars from the forward firebase was inhabited by Arabs, not Kurds.

"So even though it is on KRG territory, it's not worth losing men for," he explained. "Not until we're ready to do a much bigger offensive."

But when that offensive might come was a matter tied up with international geopolitics, and with the outcome of decisions being made in Washington and Brussels and Baghdad. In light of the woeful conduct of the Iraqi army in the past—and absent any will to place significant numbers of Western troops on the ground—many American and European politicians and foreign-policy advisers were calling for deputizing the one fighting force in the region that had proved its mettle, the Peshmerga, to lead the campaign to destroy ISIS. Less clear was whether anyone had seriously discussed this idea with the Kurds.

"You know, the Americans come here, and they want to talk about retaking Mosul," Sirwan Barzani said. "Are you going to do it with American troops? No. Are you going to do it with the Iraqi army? No, because they're useless. So let's have the Kurds do it. But what do we want with Mosul? It's not Kurdistan; it's Iraq, and why should we lose more men for the sake of Iraq?"

Animating that resistance, beyond the traditional Kurdish antipathy for the regime in Baghdad, was what the Iraqi army collapse in 2014 brought down on the KRG. The Iraqis, by abandoning their American-supplied heavy weaponry and vehicles to ISIS—in most cases, they didn't even have the presence of mind to destroy it—had virtually overnight converted the guerrilla force into one of the best-equipped armies in the region, and it was the Kurds who had paid the price. To compound matters, by the terms of the American government's prior arrangement with Iraq, even in mid-2015 all weaponry requested by the KRG in their ongoing fight with ISIS first had to be routed through Baghdad.

"Why?" Sirwan Barzani asked acidly. "So Baghdad can give even more of it to Daesh?"

By that May, the Americans were still trying to cobble together a workable arrangement. The response time for air strikes against ISIS targets had greatly improved because of the recent deployment of American aerial spotter teams in the KRG, but much slower going was the effort to forge some kind of rapprochement between the Peshmerga and the Iraqi army. Directly beside Barzani's Black Tiger Camp in Gwer was a smaller base where Iraqi soldiers were receiving American training. "I pray for the day I don't have to see that anymore," Barzani said, pointing to the Iraqi flag flying from the adjacent base.

But Black Tiger Camp revealed something else about the KRG, an aspect of the society that most of its officials, whether civilian or military, try to play down or avoid speaking about altogether. For the entire time of its existence—and indeed, far predating that—the KRG has been riven into two feuding camps, a schism that led to open civil war in the 1990s. On the surface, it has the trappings of a political duel between its two main parties, the Kurdistan Democratic Party (KDP) and the Patriotic Union of Kurdistan (PUK), but in actuality, it is a contest between two great tribal groupings, the Barzani and the Talabani. The territory's north is thoroughly dominated by the Barzanis and their tribal allies—the Mirkhans among them—virtually all of whom are KDP. Southern KRG, by contrast, is controlled by the Talabanis and their tribal allies under the PUK label.

The feudalistic nature of this arrangement was on display at Black Tiger. All the Peshmerga at the camp, and along the entire seventy-five-mile front of Sector 6, are "Barzanis," as denoted by their red-and-white tribal scarves. In the Talabani sectors of southern KRG, the Peshmerga scarves are black and white.

Further, Sirwan Barzani is the "commander" of Sector 6 less through any military acumen on his part—before the war, he was the extremely wealthy owner of a cell phone–service provider—than through the fact that he is the nephew of the KRG's president, Massoud Barzani, who in turn is the son of the legendary Kurdish warlord Mustafa Barzani. This also explains Sirwan's impolitic frankness with a foreign journalist; as a full-fledged Barzani, he is quite beyond the reach of more temperate but lesser-named KRG politicians to muzzle.

This enduring schism has had tragic consequences. In the first days of the ISIS advance into the KRG, the Peshmerga's performance was extremely shaky, and as much as they wish to fix blame for that on the prior collapse of the Iraqi army, an enormous contributing factor was that there were actually two Peshmerga armies in the field, with little in the way of coordination between them. ISIS took advantage of that to nearly capture the KRG capital, Erbil, and to start their extermination campaign against the Yazidis.

Time and again in the KRG, I detected a sense of guilt, even of shame, when conversation turned to the fate of the Yazidis. With no one, though, did I sense it more than with Azar Mirkhan. Part of that may have stemmed from his having tried to aid them at their critical hour, only to discover that the hour had come and gone. But on a philosophical level, he also felt the Kurds had betrayed their history.

"You could say that, in many ways, the Yazidis are the

pure Kurds," he explained. "Their religion is what all Kurds believed at one time, not all this Shia-Sunni business. Everyone else changed, but they stayed true to the faith."

Along with his touring of the battlefronts, Azar has spent a great deal of time at the Yazidi displaced-persons camps in northern KRG, often working with a Kurdish-Swedish doctor named Nemam Ghafouri. These camps—some run by small independent charities, some by large international relief organizations—are home to tens of thousands of the Yazidis who outran the ISIS advance of August 2014, but when I visited in May 2015, they were being joined by a handful of others who had recently either escaped or been ransomed out from ISIS control. Despite having interviewed countless war and atrocity survivors across the world over the years, I found something uniquely horrifying about these returnees' stories. It took me some time to realize this was because of what was left unsaid, the need to puzzle out in one's own mind the depravity to which they had been subjected.

ISIS had used rape and sexual slavery as a weapon of war to destroy the fabric of Yazidi society, and now that some of these girls and women were returning, the conservative Yazidi honor code didn't permit them to speak of what happened to them. In the company of Ghafouri, I met a ten-year-old girl whose extended family had raised $1,500—the savings of several lifetimes—to buy her freedom the week before. She insisted her ISIS owners had only made her clean and wash their clothes, that they never touched her, and this was a story the family was determined to believe. I met two teenage girls who had managed to escape from ISIS after just one month, along with a relative whom I took to be their mother—she looked perhaps forty-five years old, but a very hard forty-five: sunken cheeks, missing teeth, graying hair—who had been held for eight months. Except this woman wasn't their mother; she was their older sister, and she was only twenty-four. By her account, she had feigned deafness, which is seen by ISIS as a sign of mental illness, and in this way she, too, had avoided being molested.

Whatever the veracity of the eldest sister's story, I was more mystified by her younger siblings' behavior. Both were very pretty—prime candidates, it would seem, for the ISIS sex slave harem during their month-long captivity—and yet both seemed quite unaffected by their ordeal, spirited and lighthearted. Once we had left the sisters, I asked Ghafouri about it.

"No, they probably weren't raped," she explained. "In the first few weeks after the fall of Sinjar, Daesh had so many young Yazidi girls and women to choose from that they first attacked the lighter-skinned ones, those with blond hair or blue eyes. So even though both those girls are good looking, they are darker skinned, which means they were safer for a little while."

As Ghafouri explained, her mission now was to come up with some pretext to see the ten-year-old girl and the twenty-four-year-old sister alone. After winning their trust, she would conduct a physical examination. If they had, in fact, been raped, Ghafouri would inform their families that they had some sort of infection and needed to be placed in a special hospital—no visitors—for a week.

"So then they are taken to Erbil," she said. "They have

the reconstruction—it's actually a simple operation—and they come back as virgins. Then they can be accepted back; they can marry someday. Of course it also means they can never talk about what happened, they must keep it inside forever. But this is what passes for a happy ending now."

Hearing such testimonials has further hardened Azar Mirkhan's beliefs about what needs to be done if the Kurds are ever to find safety. In his view, ISIS has been only the latest in a long line of implacable Arab enemies. "If this was the first time, then maybe you could say, 'Oh, it's this horrible group of terrorists.' But this has been going on for our entire history. I can promise you that when we retake Sinjar, we will go there and we will find that the Arabs stayed with ISIS. Okay, some are here in the camps, but many more stayed. So that is why I say our enemy is not just ISIS; it's all Arabs."

29

Wakaz Hassan
Iraq

AT THE BEGINNING of June 2015, with his one-year tour of duty with ISIS drawing to a close, Wakaz conducted a reappraisal of his life. Still deployed on the battle line at the oil-refinery complex in Baiji, the young man from Dawr certainly had the option of re-upping with ISIS, but he decided instead to return to the civilian world.

Part of his reason may have involved economics; with ISIS's salad days clearly over, Wakaz's pay packet often arrived late, but it most likely was rooted even more in self-preservation. Because, slowly but surely, the tide appeared to be turning against ISIS.

This was made obvious to Wakaz as he contemplated just where he might go to start over. In April, the Iraqi army, supported by American air strikes, had recaptured the Tikrit region, including Dawr, and by that June they were closing ever tighter around Baiji. That still left Mosul and the ISIS-controlled towns in Anbar Province, but life in any of those places for an ex-ISIS fighter was sure to be grim: he would be resented by his former comrades, and a dead man should the Iraqi army win out.

Wakaz finally settled on a very different destination: the Kurdish-controlled Iraqi city of Kirkuk. For a former ISIS fighter hoping to disappear, it was a smart choice. Just as in Mosul and Baiji and Tikrit, the Iraqi army garrisoned in Kirkuk had broken and fled before the ISIS offensive the previous year, but there the similarities ended. Racing to fill the void left by the Iraqis, thousands of Peshmerga soldiers had poured into Kirkuk just ahead of ISIS and managed to throw back their advance. Ever since, Kirkuk had effectively been under Kurdish control, but the melting-pot city was also teeming with both Sunni and Shiite refugees, making it a natural hideout for both active and former Islamist fighters.

But not necessarily an easy hideout to reach. Although Kirkuk was a mere sixty miles from Baiji, the two cities were now separated by the heavily fortified line of the

Peshmerga army. It meant that, to reach his sanctuary city, Wakaz would have to travel the ISIS "ratline."

30

Majd Ibrahim
Syria · Greece

IN THE SAME month that Wakaz decided to leave ISIS, Majd finally obtained his bachelor's degree in hotel management from Al-Baath University. The achievement was a mixed blessing, for it also meant that Majd was now eligible for military conscription.

Before the war, a male student normally received his call-up letter four or five months after graduation, but by 2015, the Syrian army was so depleted from defections and battlefield casualties that the call-up time had shortened to a month or two, or even just a few weeks. What's more, there was no longer any gaming the system. So desperate was the army for fresh bodies that once the call-up notice went out, the army might simply come to your house and haul you away. "So that was it," Majd said. "I knew that in a very short time, the army would come for me."

But not if Majd's parents had any say in the matter. Just days after his graduation, they handed their son $3,000— all the savings they had left—and told Majd to leave the country.

"To them it was no longer about patriotism or defend-

Refugees off the coast of Lesbos Island, Greece, September 2015

ing the country," he said, "but about my staying alive."
He gave a faint smile. "Plus, I would have made a terrible
soldier."

On June 21, Majd's father escorted him to Damascus,
where two days later he caught a flight for Turkey. Besides
the $3,000, all Majd carried was whatever could fit into his
small knapsack.

Hoping to stay at least somewhat near home, Majd
looked for work in Turkey. When that proved futile, he saw
no choice but to join the migrant trail being negotiated
by hundreds of thousands of his countrymen that summer,
and so he headed west for Turkey's Aegean coast, where he
might seek passage to Europe. Along the way, he seren-
dipitously met up with an old friend from Homs whom
he hadn't seen in years, Amjad, who was traveling with
Ammar, another refugee from Homs. The three became a

traveling team. Consequently, they shared the same over-crowded inflatable raft that, on the night of July 27, made the passage from a smuggler's beach near the Turkish resort town of Bodrum to the Greek island of Kos, several miles away.

There, Majd and his two friends endured an agonizing wait. With Kos overwhelmed by tens of thousands of would-be migrants, Greek authorities were taking up to ten days simply to issue the registry papers that would allow their onward travel. At the same time, the migrant route through Eastern Europe was becoming increasingly inhospitable, with several governments threatening to shut it down completely. Finally, Majd and his friends received their papers late on the afternoon of August 4. That left them just enough time to catch the nightly ferry for the Greek mainland, the beginning of their search for refuge somewhere in Europe.

PART V

Exodus

2015–2016

31

Wakaz Hassan
Iraq · Syria · Turkey

ON JUNE 18, 2015, the first day of Ramadan, Wakaz bid farewell to his ISIS comrades and set off on the ISIS ratline for his return to civilian life. To reach Kirkuk, just sixty miles northeast of Baiji, Wakaz first had to travel west across ISIS-controlled Iraq and Syria, then north into Turkey, before slipping back across into Kurdish-controlled territory in northern Iraq—an almost complete circle of more than five hundred miles. The biggest potential obstacle on this well-known route was the heavily militarized Turkish frontier.

Ever since ISIS gained strength in eastern Syria in early 2014, there have been accusations that their success relied on Turkey's keeping its border deliberately porous so that both contraband and Islamist fighters from around the world might pass back and forth. That charge was made most explicitly by the Russian government in late 2015. While the Turkish administration of President Recep Tayyip Erdoğan vehemently denied the charge, the vast preponderance of evidence supports the Russian account.

In interviews with nearly two dozen captured ISIS fighters conducted for this project, at least eleven claimed to have transited through Turkey at some point during their ISIS service. Of those eleven, nine told of encountering Turkish soldiers or police while crossing the Turkish-Syrian frontier, and all were simply waved through. That was certainly the experience of Wakaz.

"There was a group of ten of us," Wakaz said, "and the man who was leading us, he went up to the Turkish checkpoint and talked to the guards for a few minutes. Maybe he gave them some money, I don't know, but then we just passed on."

As to whether there was any chance the Turkish security forces didn't grasp the affiliation of those they were letting through, Wakaz briskly shook his head. "Of course they knew. We were all young guys, and the man taking us across was Daesh. He went across there all the time. They knew."

From Turkey, Wakaz made another clandestine crossing into KRG territory, and by the beginning of July 2015, two weeks after he had left ISIS, he was in Kirkuk and ready for a fresh start. He was soon joined there by another ISIS retiree, his older brother Mohammed.

At least initially, it seemed the Hassan brothers had chosen well. In Kirkuk, they moved into a small apartment in a neighborhood favored by other ex-ISIS fighters trying to escape notice, and within a week, both brothers found work on a nearby construction site. At that point, if Wakaz had a dream for the future, it was simply to lie low in Kirkuk, save as much money as possible, and then return home when the situation permitted and open his own small shop.

As modest and heavily conditional as that dream was, it ended on the afternoon of September 7, 2015, when a black car pulled alongside Wakaz on a Kirkuk street. Rolling down his window, the man in the front passenger seat, an undercover policeman, asked the young man with the piercing eyes for his identification card.

32

Majd Ibrahim
Germany

AT 6:00 ON the evening of November 23, 2015, a crowd began to converge on the expansive open square known as Theaterplatz in central Dresden. At first, their numbers were small—just a few hundred, some carrying homemade signs or German flags—but by 7:00, the crowd had swelled to seven or eight thousand. For the next hour, they listened attentively to a succession of speakers who took to the small rostrum, applauding or waving their flags in appreciation, and then they broke to begin an orderly march through the empty streets of downtown.

Given their good manners and benign appearance—the crowd was well dressed and skewed toward early middle age—one aspect of the proceedings that the uninitiated might have found baffling was the scores of German police in riot gear who kept watch over the speechmaking in Theaterplatz, and who flanked the marchers in their progress through the streets. That gathering, however, was just the latest in a string of rallies that had taken place every Monday night in Dresden over the previous year, and which had made the city in eastern Germany one of the tensest flash points in Europe's deepening immigration crisis.

What gave Dresden a starring role in that crisis was the creation there in October 2014 of an organization called Patriotic Europeans Against the Islamization of the West, more commonly known by its German acronym, PEGIDA. An umbrella group for various German right-wing and anti-immigration groups, PEGIDA's past marches had occasionally been marked by violence, sparked both by neo-Nazis and skinheads within its ranks and by leftist counterdemonstrators. By the autumn of 2015, however, a combination of the heavy police presence and the efforts of PEGIDA leaders to purge their most extremist members had imposed a calming effect. The police kept a close watch for "hooligan" elements and anyone who appeared intoxicated, while the Theaterplatz speakers struck a civil tone. Still, the immigrant and minority communities of Dresden knew to stay well away from downtown on Monday nights. This included a rather recent arrival to the city from Syria, twenty-three-year-old Majd Ibrahim.

From Greece, Majd and his two companions from Homs, Amjad and Ammar, had traveled the migrant trail through Eastern Europe and reached southern Germany by mid-August. Majd had intended to continue on alone to Sweden, where he'd heard winning asylum was easiest, but those plans were dashed when the three friends were pulled off a northbound train by German police. After being shunted between different migrant holding facilities, they were brought to Dresden in mid-September. There, the local social-welfare agency had placed the Syrians in a small attic apartment on the outskirts of town, shared with six other asylum seekers, as they waited for their petitions for resident status to wend their way through the German legal system.

For refugees from Homs to find themselves in Dresden held a certain paradox. The city, infamous for having been largely destroyed by Allied bombing in World War II, lay in what until 1989 had been East Germany, and it was in the east where the anti-immigration movement had taken deepest root since German unification. That discontent had reached a new boiling point amid the migrant crisis in the summer of 2015, when close to a million would-be refugees had flooded into Europe—the majority from Syria and Iraq, and the majority making for Germany. In Dresden and other eastern German towns where the migrants were housed, that had translated into isolated beatings of migrants and arson attacks on their shelters. When I visited Majd on November 23, it had been just a week since terrorist strikes in Paris killed 130, and anger against the migrants—and especially any from Muslim countries—was at a new fever pitch.

"There have been quite a few incidents here just this past week," Majd told me. "A lot of the guys won't go to the city center at all right now."

Certainly they wouldn't be heading downtown that evening, a Monday, when the PEGIDA activists were gathering in Theaterplatz.

But against this atmosphere of tension, Majd and his Syrian companions had developed an easy camaraderie with the other migrants in the attic apartment. Meals had become a new preoccupation, and two of their roommates, from India, had installed themselves as the lords of the kitchen.

"Their food is much better than ours," Majd explained. "They give us a list of what to buy, and we go to the market for them, but they do almost all of the cooking."

As he waited for his asylum petition to work its way through the German bureaucracy, Majd passed the time taking German-language classes offered by the local university and trying to stay in touch with his family and friends back in Syria through Facebook and the occasional telephone call. What he didn't spend a lot of time doing was monitoring the situation in his homeland, especially all the talk about cease-fires or foreign-brokered peace talks; he had been optimistic so many times before, only to see the fighting resume, that he now refused to get his hopes up at all. Plus, he simply saw no way out of the morass.

"The militant groups will never agree to a peace where Assad stays in power, but what happens if Assad is forced out? Then not only are the Alawites finished, but so are the Christians and the Ismailis [a moderate Shiite splinter sect] and anyone else who isn't Sunni. So that is why I think Assad is the best out of all bad choices. With anyone else, I think Syria is destroyed forever."

Majd had spoken frequently of his intention to return

to Syria someday, and that afternoon I asked if he could foresee a time when such a return would be possible. He thought for a long time. "Minimum, ten years from now," he said. "We have a saying in Syria: 'Blood brings blood.' Now everyone will want to take revenge for what has been done to them these past years, so it will just go on and on. Blood brings blood. I don't think it will end until everyone who has taken up a gun in this war is dead. Even if the killing speeds up, that will still take at least ten years."

By coincidence, I was with Majd the following day, when, returning to his communal apartment, he found a letter awaiting him. It was from the Federal Office for Migration and Refugees, and it informed Majd that a background check on him had just been completed and that no problems were found; it was the last major hurdle in his petition for residency, making it all but certain that Majd would now be allowed to stay in Germany for the next three years. Setting the letter aside, the college student from Homs crossed to one of the attic's dormer windows and sat staring out at the street for a long time.

33

Khulood al-Zaidi
Jordan · Greece · Austria

BY THE END of 2015, Khulood had come up with a desperate plan. Her years of petitioning for resettlement having gone nowhere, she now saw absolutely no future for her family in Jordan. All that summer and autumn, she had been following the story of the hundreds of thousands of prospective migrants making for Europe from Turkey—and, far more perilously, from Libya—aboard flimsy inflatable rafts. By December, however, it was a rapidly changing story; more and more restrictions were being placed on the migrants by European governments, and, with winter coming on, the sea passage was becoming increasingly risky. As Khulood explained to her father and sisters, if ever they were to change their situation, they had to act immediately.

With Ali al-Zaidi's health too precarious to withstand the rigors of a hard journey, it was decided that Sahar would remain with him in Amman while Khulood and Teamim made for Europe. On December 4, they took a flight to Istanbul and from there followed the by now well-worn migrant trail down the Turkish coast to the city of Izmir.

After arranging to pay a smuggler two thousand euros for spots aboard a boat, the sisters waited for word on when they might sail. The summons finally came on the night of December 11.

They were driven an hour and a half down the coast. Slipping to the shoreline in the darkness, Khulood and Teamim clambered aboard a severely overloaded rubber raft—Khulood counted at least thirty other passengers, rather than the eight or ten it was designed to hold—which then pushed off for the Greek island of Samos, a three-hour journey.

The overburdened raft lay so low in the water that twice the outboard motor died when waves broke over it, but the greatest danger came when they had nearly reached safety. On the murky sliver-moon night, the pilot misgauged his approach to the Samos beach and smashed the raft against a rock outcropping; instantly, one of the air-filled pontoons began to collapse. Ready to join the other passengers tumbling into the water from the sinking boat—fortunately, all wore life preservers—Khulood thought to glance over at Teamim. Her oldest sister sat stock-still, too paralyzed with fear to react.

"I yelled at her to jump," Khulood recalled, "because the waves were very high and they were going to smash us against the rocks, but she just couldn't move. I saw that she was going to die, but I thought, 'We've come too far together, we must now share our fate.'"

Clambering over to her sister, Khulood grabbed Teamim and somehow managed to get them both clear of the sinking vessel and onto the rocks. There they were promptly

A Syrian refugee collapsing in the heat in Mytilene, Greece, September 2015

knocked down by another wave, with Teamim badly hurting her leg in the fall, but at least they were now on land. In the dark, Khulood helped her limping sister up the hillside to join the rest of the migrants as they set out in search of shelter.

The following two weeks became a blur of travel and waiting and tension for the two sisters from Iraq, an abject lesson in both the callous indifference of officialdom and in the life-altering kindness of strangers. After registering with Greek authorities in Samos, the sisters were allowed to board a ferryboat for the Greek mainland and Athens, where they were taken in by a friend of a friend. With the situation at the Eastern European frontiers changing almost by the day—and not in any way that augured well for the thousands of migrants still streaming north—the sisters quickly moved on. By December 22, through a combination of bus, train, and foot travel, Khulood and Teamim had crossed five European borders to finally reach southern Germany.

There, their luck appeared to run out. Arrested shortly after crossing the German frontier, the sisters were held in jail until dark, then sent back into Austria and instructed to make for a refugee holding center in the town of Klagenfurt. That camp was so filled to overflowing, however, that they were denied entry. With nowhere else to go, Khulood and Teamim simply huddled together outside the camp's gates—and then it began to snow.

Their salvation was arranged through social media. After Khulood posted notice of their situation on Facebook, a small international band of activists mobilized in search of someone in the Klagenfurt area who might help the sisters. That aid soon arrived in the form of a local Green member of parliament, who took Khulood and Teamim to a café to eat and warm up. At the café, the politician also sent out an urgent message seeking a local family who might temporarily take in the sisters; within the hour, he had received eight offers. From the café, the Zaidi sisters were taken to the home of Elisabeth and Erich Edelsbrunner.

"Today is the first day we feel comfortable and relaxed," Khulood e-mailed a friend in England the following day, Christmas Eve. "The family is very nice. They have given us our own room. They have a very lovely dog. I love him."

34

Wakaz Hassan
Iraq

IN DECEMBER 2015, Wakaz Hassan was being kept in a small former police station at the edge of a village about ten miles from Kirkuk. Along with approximately forty other men being held as suspected terrorists, the former ISIS fighter, now twenty-one, spent almost all his waking hours kneeling in a small and fetid room of the secret prison run by the KRG's security service, Asayish. On those rare occasions when Wakaz was taken from the communal room, he was handcuffed and blindfolded, with the blindfold only removed when he was securely within another featureless room of the prison compound. In this way, he still had no idea where he was even after three months of captivity.

After being picked up on the streets of Kirkuk in September, Wakaz quickly confessed to having been an ISIS fighter. He provided details of his service, including the six executions he carried out in Mosul. Whether this confession was coerced through torture was impossible to know—in conversation with me in the prison, Wakaz insisted that the Asayish interrogators hadn't mistreated him in any way, but even tortured prisoners tend to say that when their captors are standing over them. Over the course of our two long interviews, the young man sometimes contradicted himself, perhaps a result of trying to gauge what his questioner and captors might want to hear. That said, there seemed a core candor to his words that perhaps was at least partly due to a stricken conscience.

"I did bad things," he told me, "and I need to confess to them before God."

Shortly after his arrest, Wakaz also informed on his brother Mohammed. It took Asayish a month to track down the older Hassan sibling, and he was being held in a different prison near Kirkuk. There had been no contact between the brothers since their arrests, but Wakaz hoped Mohammed was also making a clean slate of things. His main goal now, he said, was to atone for his crimes by helping the authorities identify whichever of his former ISIS comrades were still alive. "If I had a chance to do it over again," he said, "I never would have joined Daesh. I saw the evil things they did, and I know now that they aren't true Muslims."

Despite this professed change of heart, the twenty-one-year-old is clear-eyed about his future. "I have no illusions, and I have no hope," he told me. "I believe I will spend the rest of my life in prison."

But Wakaz was basing that belief on the fact that he had been captured by KRG investigators and remained in Kurdish custody. In reality, a grimmer future was being planned for Wakaz, one plainly laid out to me by a senior Asayish officer at the secret prison.

Since the events of June 2014—when the Iraqi army in

Men mourning in Balad, Iraq, 2016

Kirkuk melted away before the ISIS assault, and the Kurds rushed into the breach—the city has technically been under the joint control of the Iraqis and the Kurds. But this collaboration exists largely on paper. In practice, the Kurdish authorities have little faith in their Iraqi counterparts and see even less reason to cooperate with them on security matters. Nowhere is this separation more evident than on issues relating to ISIS.

"That's why we haven't told the Iraqis about the guys in here," explained the Asayish official. "If we did, they would demand we hand them over, since most of their crimes were committed on Iraqi territory. Then they would either kill these guys outright or, if some of them are high enough up in the Daesh leadership to arrange a bribe, let them go. We just can't trust the Iraqis at all." In light of that, the Asayish plan is to keep Wakaz under wraps and to use him to identify other ISIS fighters they capture and with whom he might have served in the field. Once his usefulness to Asayish comes to an end—and that may not be until after the retaking of Mosul and the trove of ISIS fighters expected to surrender there—Wakaz will be handed over to the Iraqi authorities. At that point, his future will be short and preordained.

"He thinks his life will be saved because we have him, and he knows we don't execute," the Asayish officer said. "But Iraq does. The Iraqis will try him in their courts here, and they will give him a death sentence. Then they will transfer him to one of the prisons in Iraq where they do the executions, and he will be hanged."

When I asked if there was any chance that, because of Wakaz's assistance in unmasking other ISIS fighters, a judge might show leniency in his case, the Asayish officer quickly shook his head. Or that he could somehow cut a deal to spare his life? The officer pondered briefly, then shook his head even more forcefully.

"If he was senior Daesh, maybe," he said. "But he is a nobody and poor. So no. No chance."

35

Majdi el-Mangoush
Libya

ON A MORNING in early March 2016, Majdi el-Mangoush and I drove out of Misurata for the farm fields and small villages at its southern outskirts. He wanted to show me the forest that he and a group of local conservationists tended. Three years earlier, Majdi had become involved with an environmental group based in Tripoli called Tree Lovers and had been so inspired by their work that he had helped start a Misurata branch. While both money and supplies are tight, the volunteers have planted flowers and shrubs along many of the city's dusty median strips and sought to raise awareness about the importance of preserving the very little vegetation Libya possesses.

"With climate change, it's even more important," Majdi said. "The desert is spreading in lots of places in Libya, and the only way to stop that is with trees."

After receiving his sham diploma in communications engineering from the Libyan government in 2012, the former air force cadet had faced a stark choice: he could use that piece of paper to land some inconsequential government job, or Majdi could start over. The following year, he had enrolled in Misurata University to study engineering, and by 2016 was finally close to receiving a degree that actually meant something.

All around him, though, he saw a country that was not just stagnating but going backward. For the first two years of the post-Qaddafi era, Libya had enjoyed at least the appearance of a central and democratic government, the General National Congress (GNC), but that had ended in mid-2014 when, following a failed military coup, two rival governments were established. With Islamist groups taking over the GNC in Tripoli—they soon renamed it the Government of National Salvation—a competing regime, the Council of Deputies, decamped for the eastern Libyan port town of Tobruk. As might be predicted, the two rival administrations soon had their own lineup of competing outside benefactors, with Qatar and Turkey leading regional support for the Islamist-dominated regime, while the United States and most Western European nations insisted the Tobruk organization was the legitimate one—never mind that, for a time, its authority barely extended beyond its seat of government: a leased Greek car ferry moored in Tobruk Harbor.

As might also be predicted, into this power vacuum stepped the Middle East's radical militias. By late 2014, groups operating under the ISIS umbrella had taken over a vast stretch of Libya's central coast, culminating in their seizure of the city of Sirte in early 2015. By the end of that year, thousands of ISIS fighters threatened to turn the North African nation into a new *terrorist internationale.*

Coming terribly late to the game, Western powers began bombing purported ISIS encampments in Libya in February 2016, actions that by then did little more than drive deeper wedges between the country's dizzying array of regional factions and tribal militias.

For Majdi, there had also recently been a more personal reminder of the capriciousness of war, of how what separates the living from the dead is often a matter of luck or connections. During our drive out through the farmlands, he was recounting the story of his escape from the clutches of the Qaddafi regime when I thought to ask after the fate of Ayoub, the regime spy handler he had double-crossed in Misurata. I fully expected to hear the man had been placed before a rebel firing squad, but instead Majdi gave a caustic chuckle, shook his head. "Not at all," he said. "I saw him on Tunisian television just last month. He's become a political pundit."

But along with its governmental crisis, Libya is now hurtling toward an economic brick wall. Incredible as it might seem amid the chaos of the past few years, the Libyan national bank has continued to pay the salaries and pensions of the 50 percent of Libyans who were on the government payroll during Qaddafi's reign. Among these is Majdi el-Mangoush. "Because of my time in the air force," he explained. "Even though I have no duties, I'm still officially a reservist, so every month I get a paycheck for that."

Along with this staggering payroll, another carryover from the Qaddafi era is a broad array of economic subsidies; gasoline, for example, remains just seven cents a gallon. The most tangible result is the transformation of Libya into the world's largest fire-sale bazaar, with huge quantities of its subsidized products smuggled across its borders to be resold in Tunisia or Egypt. So vast is this outflow that entire fishing fleets along the coast have been converted into oil- and gasoline-smuggling vessels, simultaneously causing fish to all but disappear from local markets and ensuring that the Libyan oil industry actually loses money for every barrel of oil it produces. In tandem with the collapse of world oil prices, this phenomenon has helped accelerate the emptying of Libya's hard currency reserves. By best esti- mate, those reserves—standing at $110 billion as recently as 2013—had already been reduced to $43 billion by late 2016, with the zero mark likely to be reached sometime in 2017. Yet, within Libya there is little sign of any will to confront this approaching calamity. To the contrary; with most of the rival militias and political factions having a hand in the looting, there is a powerful incentive to let it continue.

In contemplating the series of vicious circles that have engulfed his homeland, Majdi el-Mangoush has turned to a novel idea: a restoration of the monarchy that Qaddafi overthrew in 1969. "Not that it will solve all our prob- lems," he said, "but at least with the king we were a nation, we had an identity. Without that identity, we are all just individuals—or at most, members of a tribe."

If Majdi's proposal seems a naive one, it's actually rooted in a kind of pragmatic despair; unless some unifying force like the monarchy is introduced, he fears, the dissolution of Libya will merely accelerate. "And it won't just be the split between Tripolitania and Cyrenaica that everyone talks about," he said. "It will then go to the tribal and provincial level, because once you start with divisions here, there's no natural place to stop." Off the top of his head, Majdi listed six major ethnic or tribal fault lines in Libya, six potential future statelets—and even that number, he suggested, was probably conservative. "So that is why I believe we need the monarchy back. When I first started saying this to my friends a couple of years ago, they just laughed, but now more and more people are thinking this way."

After about an hour's drive into the countryside below Misurata, Majdi turned the car onto a narrow farm road and stopped. One of the more intriguing phenomena observed among ex-soldiers most everywhere is a desire for solitude, to be out in nature. Majdi clearly shares this impulse, but in the arid lands of Libya, that means making do. His "forest" proved to be little more than a few rows of scraggly pines set beside the farm road, with trash strewn about from careless picnickers, but Majdi was very happy there. Stepping around the garbage, he strolled among the trees and breathed in deeply of the pine scent with a satisfied smile.

"Okay, it isn't Jebel Akhdar," he said, referring to the Green Mountain region he had visited with his friend Jalal, "but at least it's a beginning."

36

Laila Soueif
Egypt

IN JANUARY 2016, Laila's son, Alaa, managed to smuggle an open letter to *The Guardian* from his Egyptian prison cell. "It has been months since I wrote a letter and more than a year since I've written an article. I have nothing to say: no hopes, no dreams, no fears, no warnings, no insights; nothing, absolutely nothing," he wrote. "I try to remember what it was like when tomorrow seemed so full of possibility and my words seemed to have the power to influence (if only slightly) what that tomorrow would look like. I can't really remember that."

By then, Alaa was approaching the one-year mark of a five-year prison sentence, just as his father, now deceased, had predicted. It was a high price for speaking out, and one of the awful paradoxes Alaa faced—along with the tens of thousands of other political prisoners in Egypt today—was that the old way of appealing to Cairo on human rights issues no longer worked. In the Mubarak era, if enough pressure was brought to bear by the American government and Western activist groups, an Egyptian political prisoner was likely to be quietly released. If General Sisi took away any lesson from Mubarak's downfall, though, it was to never be viewed as the West's lapdog. As a result, outside pressure applied today has little effect, and might even be counterproductive.

"But of course, you also can't stay quiet about it," Laila said, "because this is exactly what they want. You have to keep trying, even if it seems futile."

The obduracy of the Sisi regime on human rights has undoubtedly been compounded by a new economic reality. Today, the annual American subsidy to Egypt is less than $1.3 billion, down from more than $2 billion in Mubarak's heyday. At the same time, Saudi Arabia and other gulf states have subsidized the Egyptian government with an estimated $30 billion since Sisi took power, and given the Saudis' own record on such matters, they seem unlikely to pester their client state over issues like political prisoners or freedom of expression. The simple fact is that the West in general, and the United States in particular, now has less influence over the Egyptian state than at any time since the early 1970s.

Laila derives some perverse hope from the recent economic deterioration of Egypt, a decline so rapid and deep that it might, she believes, finally erode all remaining trust in the present regime. "Sisi still has pools of support," she said, "but it's getting smaller all the time. The situation is really unsustainable now. At a certain point, the argument, 'But he saved us from the terrorists,' won't work anymore."

But in March 2016, there were scant signs in Cairo or elsewhere in Egypt that any serious dissident movement was in the offing. "No, it won't happen today, and it won't be like Tahrir," Laila said. "I give it eighteen months. In eighteen months, either there will be a kind of palace coup—the generals put Sisi to one side and bring in some-one more moderate—or we will come to a new wave of widespread protest. If that happens, it won't be like 2011. This time, it will be far more violent."

The Sisi regime shows few signs of being worried. A sec-ond case against Alaa, for criticizing the justice system on his Facebook page, is currently in court, and he faces the possibility of another sentence of six months to three years. Even if prosecutors drop that case, Laila will be sixty-four when her son is released.

37

Azar Mirkhan
Kurdistan

AT THE SIGHT of the Arab village on the road just ahead, Azar Mirkhan brought the car to a quick stop and swore under his breath in Kurdish. It was a poor and tattered place: off to the left, a compact cluster of earthen homes and walls and, to the right, four or five farmhouses climbing the hillside. It was the latter grouping that drew the doctor's attention.

"They're on the high ground? How was that allowed?" Azar stared darkly at the farmhouses for a moment, seething at the Arab encroachment, then slowly turned his gaze to the village center. No residents were visible, but here and there old cars were parked in the shadow of walls.

"You see? Until two weeks ago, Daesh controlled this village, and the people living here had no problem with them, they stayed throughout. We lost four Peshmerga here." Azar turned to me with his lopsided, grim smile. "You know what I would do? I would go to an Arab and ask to borrow his bulldozer. Then I'd bring in an Israeli adviser—they're very good at this sort of thing—and in two or three days, I would erase this place."

Azar has a flair for the outrageous statement, and I sometimes found it hard to know how serious he really was with such proclamations. But on that morning, I suspected he was quite sincere. It was November 27, 2015, six months after my first visit with Azar, and we were on a back road to Sinjar, the Yazidi town that ISIS had so thoroughly savaged in the summer of 2014. In the intervening months, Azar had occasionally driven out to the Peshmerga frontline trench above Sinjar to try his hand at shooting ISIS fighters—occupying an opposing trench just forty yards away—but the Peshmerga, with the help of massive American air strikes, had recently recaptured the town itself. Azar had participated in that battle, and this return trip put him in a dark mood.

His ill temper only deepened when we reached Sinjar. Much of the town, home to perhaps one hundred thousand before the war, had been reduced to rubble. While still checking for booby traps, the Peshmerga had cleared a narrow path through the ruins, and here and there lay the putrefying remains of a few ISIS fighters. So great was the damage that it was initially difficult to differentiate between what had been destroyed by the marauding ISIS warriors during their occupation and what had been leveled in the battle two weeks earlier, but a pattern emerged. In the small traffic circle at the center of town, ISIS had blown up the minaret that had stood there for more than eight hundred years. They had also razed every Yazidi temple in Sinjar, along with its one Christian church. The hospital in the center of town still stood, but only because ISIS converted it into a sniper's nest and barracks, knowing that American warplanes wouldn't bomb it. Even so, they had taken the time to destroy all the medical equipment, even stomping on thermometers and glass ampoules.

It was in Sinjar's residential neighborhoods, however, where ISIS's policy of ethnic cleansing took on an Old Testament air. On street after street, some houses remained perfectly intact, alongside others reduced to piles of broken masonry and twisted rebar. What most of the surviving houses had in common were spray-painted messages on their exterior walls, each something to the effect of "An Arab family lives here." Azar insisted that these were written not by the ISIS invaders but by the Arab families themselves.

"This was their message to Daesh," he said. " 'Spare us, we are with you, we aren't Kurds.' And just like in that village, the Arabs stayed here throughout."

Those Arab residents were now gone, having fled when

A mosque used by ISIS as an arms depot after an American air strike,
Tikrit, Iraq, July 2016

American air strikes signaled the coming battle. On several
of the residential streets, some of the few Yazidis who had
returned were picking their way through the Arab homes,
loading looted bedding and furniture into pickup trucks.

"And why not?" Azar said. "They have lost everything."

It all became far more visceral and ghastly when two Peshmerga fighters led us to a barren field a short distance out of
town, near the new front lines. At the far end of the field,
Peshmerga engineers were cutting a new tank trench—
ISIS remained just a few miles to the south—but farther
up, three irregular mounds flanked a seasonal water runoff. From these mounds protruded the telltale evidence of a
killing field: human bones and skulls, dirt-encrusted shoes,
loops of tied cloth that had been blindfolds. In the rains over

the previous fifteen months, some of the remains of the mass graves had leached out so that the dry streambed was littered with women's clothes, more shoes, teeth. None of the graves had been excavated yet—the authorities were waiting for a criminal forensics team—but by best estimates, this had been the execution ground for about three hundred Yazidis, most of them women too elderly to be of sex-slave interest to ISIS or children too young to be put to any use.

For a half hour, Azar walked among the graves in silence, but I noticed he was becoming increasingly agitated and then that he was crying. I drew alongside to ask if he was okay, if he wanted to leave. He abruptly wheeled to point a finger at the steeply rising flank of Mount Sinjar, maybe four miles to the north.

"The Peshmerga were right up there," the doctor said, his voice ragged with rage. "They brought them out here to kill so that we could watch. They thought about it. They did it deliberately, to humiliate us."

Returning to the center of Sinjar, Azar strode briskly into the town hall, one of the few downtown structures still habitable, and motioned for a senior official to follow him out to the terrace. For the next hour, the two men huddled in deep conversation, waving away any Peshmerga underlings who thought to approach. Afterward, Azar apologized to me for having taken so long.

"I told him that he needed to destroy all the Arab homes here," he recounted, "but he was hesitant. He thinks it's better to give them to the Yazidis who return, but I said, 'No; eventually some of those Arabs will come back with their titles and deeds and try to reclaim the houses, so better to just destroy them, leave nothing for them to come back to and start over again.' He understands that now."

When I asked if he thought the official would actually follow through with the plan, Azar nodded. "He promised me. I made him promise."

That afternoon, we climbed the hairpin road that led out of town and up Mount Sinjar, the same path that tens of thousands of terrorized Yazidis had taken in their panicked flight of August 2014. All along the shoulders of the road were clumps of the clothes, faded and torn, that they had cast aside as they ran.

"There used to be a lot more," Azar muttered as he looked at the detritus. "It used to be everywhere."

Cresting the mountain, we entered a broad valley plateau that extended for the next twenty-five miles. Scattered over the land were the tent encampments of thousands of Yazidi families that still had no homes to return to. The historic heart of Yazidi society wasn't the lowlands these people had so recently fled but rather the very mountain on which they were now camped, and on the hillsides all around their tent cities were the remnants of their ancestral villages, old abandoned crop terraces, and crumbling earthen homes. Some of these settlements had been inhabited for nearly a thousand years, but in the 1970s, Saddam Hussein sent his soldiers in to destroy them as part of his anti-Kurd campaign. The mountain Yazidis had then been herded down to the lowlands where they could be more easily watched—and, of course, more easily slaughtered when ISIS rolled in four decades later.

Until a short time ago, Azar might have been derided as a xenophobe, even a fascist, for his radical separatist views. In seeing the results of ISIS's barbarism, however, and in contemplating the hatreds that have been unleashed across the Middle East in the past few years, some observers have begun to believe that his hard way of thinking might offer the best—or, more accurately, only—path out of the morass. Indeed, it's a sign of the despair over finding any other approach that might reassemble the shattered nations of the region that has caused an ever-increasing number of diplomats and generals and policymakers to consider just the sort of ethnic and sectarian separation that Azar advocates, albeit in less brutal form.

Coincidentally, the model they most often look to for how it can be done right is the Kurdistan Regional Government.

For twenty-five years, the KRG has existed as a stable quasi democracy, part of Iraq in name only. Perhaps the answer is to replicate that model for the rest of Iraq, to create a trifurcated nation rather than the currently bifurcated one. Give the Sunnis their own "Sunni Regional Government," with all the accoutrements the Kurds already enjoy: a head of state, internal borders, an autonomous military and civil government. Iraq could still exist on paper, and a mechanism could be instituted to ensure that oil revenue is equitably divided among the three—and if it works in Iraq, perhaps this is a future solution for a balkanized Libya or a disintegrated Syria.

Even proponents acknowledge that such separations would not be easy. What to do with the thoroughly "mixed" populations of cities like Baghdad or Aleppo? In Iraq, many tribes are divided into Shia and Sunni subgroups, and in Libya by geographic dispersions going back centuries. Do these people choose to go with tribe or sect or homeland? In fact, parallels in history suggest that such a course would be both wrenching and murderous—witness the postwar "de-Germanization" policy in Eastern Europe and the 1947 partition of the Indian subcontinent—but despite the misery and potential body count entailed in getting there, maybe this is the last, best option available to prevent the failed states of the Middle East from devolving into even more brutal slaughter.

The problem, though, is that once such subdividing begins, it's hard to see where it would end. Just beneath the ethnic and religious divisions that the Iraq invasion and the Arab Spring tore open are those of tribe and clan and subclan—and in this respect, the Kurdistan Regional Government appears not so much a model but a warning.

Because of its two feuding tribes, the KRG—a statelet the size of West Virginia—now has essentially two of everything: two leaders, two governments, two armies. For the moment, this schism has been masked by the threat from ISIS and the desire to present a unified front to the outside world, but it remains an undercurrent to everything. It also goes a long way toward explaining the sad fate of the Yazidis. As Azar pointed out, any fool could see exactly where ISIS was headed in August 2014, but because the Yazidis existed outside the KRG power structure, because they had no traditional alliance with either rival faction, they were left to largely fend for themselves. For all the excuses offered up by KRG politicians and generals, the undeniable fact is that Sinjar simply wouldn't have happened if its residents had been named Barzani or Talabani.

And what happens in the KRG when the current danger subsides? If history is a guide, the Barzani-Talabani schism will worsen and may even lead to another civil war, for part of the hidden history of this place is the series of internecine wars the tribes have waged ever since they first came into contact, a legacy of mutual bloodletting dating back at least half a century and extending to as recently as the mid-1990s. It's a hidden history that the Mirkhan family knows from personal experience.

Over the course of many conversations with the various Mirkhan brothers, I heard a great deal about the exploits and personalities of the two family members who lost their lives as Peshmerga and who have now entered the pantheon of Kurdish martyrs: their father, Heso, and their brother Ali. What I heard little about—and the brothers' reticence on this topic became increasingly striking—were the actual circumstances of their deaths. It was only after repeated prodding that Azar finally divulged what I'd already ascertained independently: rather than by the Kurds' myriad external enemies, both Heso and Ali Mirkhan were actually killed by rival Kurdish Peshmerga.

"It's a disgrace that Kurds should kill each other," Azar offered when I asked why he'd been so reluctant to share the information. "With all the other enemies we have, how can we ever turn on each other?"

An excellent question, but it is one likely to be asked again and again all across a partitioned Middle East, no matter how far down those divisions and subdivisions are made.

At about the midpoint on the Sinjar plateau, a bend in the road suddenly revealed an exquisite village on the far side of the river: a series of houses climbing the rocky hillside and, just below them, a number of ancient stone terraces. Some of the terrace walls were more than twenty feet high, the inhabitants determined to carve out any little piece of workable land from the mountain, and, built in an age before machines, they must have taken years—decades, perhaps—to erect. The homes were deserted now, their roofs caved in by Saddam Hussein's soldiers, but they had left the terraces alone.

"It must have been so beautiful here then," Azar said, gazing up at the village, "a kind of garden."

But for Azar, the past was most useful for what it said about the future, and putting Sinjar behind us had set him in a happier, anticipatory mood. As we continued across the mountain, he drummed his fingers on the steering wheel.

"This is our time now," he said. "Iraq is gone. Syria is gone. Now it is our time."

EPILOGUE

AFTER SIXTEEN MONTHS traveling in the Middle East, I find it impossible to predict what might happen next, let alone sum up what it all means. In most every place Paolo Pellegrin and I went, the situation today looks worse than it did when we set out—the repression of the Sisi regime in Egypt has deepened; the war in Syria has taken tens of thousands more lives; to add to its other problems, Libya is now hurtling toward insolvency. If there is one bright spot on the map, it is the slow but seemingly inexorable defeat of ISIS in Iraq. Following the recapture of the cities of Ramadi and Fallujah earlier in 2016, an unlikely coalition of the Iraqi army, Shiite militias, and the Kurdish Peshmerga launched an assault on the ISIS bastion of Mosul in October. When Mosul falls, it will also effectively end the ISIS "caliphate" in Iraq.

That said, I am reminded of something Majd Ibrahim told me: "ISIS isn't just an organization, it's an idea." It is also a kind of tribe, of course, and even if this incarnation is destroyed, the conditions that created ISIS will remain in the form of a generation of disaffected and futureless young men, like Wakaz Hassan, who find purpose and power and belonging by picking up a gun. In sum, nothing gets better anytime soon.

But how much worse it gets might also depend largely on external forces, and specifically on how the new American administration responds to events in the Middle East. If agonizingly slow in coming, one of the crowning achievements of the Obama administration was its methodical building of the international military coalition now confronting ISIS, a coalition that paradoxically includes some of the same nations—Turkey, Saudi Arabia—that once helped the terror group flourish. In looking beyond the crisis of the moment, perhaps the best hope for the wider region is that this international coalition not only extends into the future but takes on a broader political and humanitarian role, one that will enable it to respond more quickly and effectively to the new crises sure to come.

But to achieve that will require both hard work and diplomacy, and the initial signs of this being taken up by the isolationist-minded Trump administration are not at all encouraging. Even more worrisome has been Trump's vitriolic bombast about "Islamic terrorism." One of the most striking patterns I found on this journey was that, of the nearly two dozen former ISIS fighters I interviewed, only one professed to have joined for religious reasons. All the rest enlisted for the most banal of reasons: money, prestige, because their buddies had joined. In essence, then, it seems that what primarily drives young Arab men to ISIS is very similar to what might drive a disaffected American youth

Girl running in Tikrit, Iraq, 2016

to an inner-city gang, or a young Mexican to the *narcos*, and that combating the danger they pose is more of a sociological and economic undertaking than an ideological one. Perversely, with its veiled talk of a war between religions, the Trump administration has adopted the very same rhetoric peddled by ISIS—and if that is a war the administration wants to have, ISIS leaders will surely do all they can to provide it.

On a more philosophical level, this journey has served to remind me again of how terribly delicate is the fabric of civilization, of the vigilance required to protect it, and of the slow and painstaking work of mending it once it has been torn. This is hardly an original thought; it is a lesson we were supposed to have learned after Nazi Germany, after Bosnia and Rwanda. Perhaps it is a lesson we need to constantly relearn.

Against this, I found solace in the extraordinary power of the individual to bring change, and no person that I met more exemplified this than Khulood al-Zaidi. Through sheer force of will, Khulood—the youngest daughter of a traditional family in a provincial city in Iraq—became an unlikely yet remarkable leader, and in the process saved what she could of her family. Here, too, though, is a paradox. It is people like Khulood who must see to the mending of these fractured lands, yet it is those very people, the best their nations have to offer, who are leaving in search of a better life elsewhere. Today, Austria's gain is Iraq's loss.

AS I WRITE this, the battle for Mosul remains joined. For Dr. Azar Mirkhan, however, the true struggle, of fully separating his Kurdish homeland from the Arab world, will continue in the battle's aftermath. That aftermath will also mark the end of Wakaz Hassan's usefulness to his captors; as bluntly explained by the Kurdish security officer, he will then almost surely be handed over to Iraqi authorities for execution, if he has not been already.

In Libya, Majdi el-Mangoush is continuing his engineering studies in his hometown of Misurata. In December 2016, a motley amalgam of militias finally succeeded in driving ISIS from the coastal city of Sirte, but fighting still rages elsewhere. The one consensus about Libya, held by natives and outside observers alike, is that the nation faces a very long and hard road back to some semblance of normality. On that road, Majdi believes he has a role to play.

"I want to help my country return," he told me. "Libya is a wonderful place. More, it is my home, and I don't want to leave it for anything. Yes, the future is full of uncertainty, but so was the past. I am ready for a new kind of uncertainty."

In Dresden, Majd Ibrahim has been granted refugee status, which will enable him to remain in Germany for at least the next three years. Having become proficient in German, he was recently hired on as the night auditor at the Holiday Inn in Dresden.

In Egypt, Laila Soueif's son, Alaa, is now completing the second year of his five-year prison sentence. Laila's youngest daughter, Sanaa, was released in September 2015 under a presidential pardon, after having served fifteen months, but that didn't end her troubles with the Sisi regime. In May 2016, Sanaa was found guilty of "insulting the judiciary" for failing to answer a prosecutor's request for an interview and given a new six-month prison sentence. While some observers believe that the regime is specifically targeting Laila Soueif's family for their outspokenness, there is grim evidence that this actually might not be the case; according to a recent study by the Arabic Network for Human Rights Information (ANHRI), today an outright majority of Egypt's national prison population—estimated at 109,000—are incarcerated for political offenses.

In Austria, Khulood and her sister Teamim continue to live with the Edelsbrunner family and were recently awarded scholarships to study intercultural management at a local university. Not long ago, their mother, Aziza, who had never left Iraq and whom Khulood had seen only once since she fled Iraq twelve years ago, died in Kut. Khulood's response to the news was typical of this dauntless woman. She redoubled her efforts to rescue her remaining family, the father and sister still stranded in Jordan, and bring them to Austria. "To bring them here, to have a family again," she said. "That is my greatest dream."

ACKNOWLEDGMENTS

IN THE AUTUMN of 2014, I was approached by Jake Silverstein, the editor in chief of *The New York Times Magazine*, with the idea of producing a comprehensive report on the current upheavals in the Middle East. He sweetened the deal by suggesting that, if what I produced was compelling enough, he might devote an entire issue of the magazine to my findings. As a result, much of what appears in these pages first ran in the August 14, 2016, issue of *The New York Times Magazine*, and for granting me that unprecedented opportunity—certainly the high point of my journalistic career—I am forever in Jake's debt.

I would also like to thank my story editor at *The New York Times*, Luke Mitchell, for so tirelessly and painstakingly shepherding that project to fruition, as well as Ilena Silverman and Bill Wasik for their sage advice and editorial suggestions. As well, I am deeply appreciative of the magazine's crack fact-checking team—David Ferguson, Dan Kaufman, and Steven Stern—who time and again saved me from my own mistakes. For their generous financial support of this project, and for helping it reach an even wider audience, I am deeply grateful to Jon Sawyer and Fareed Mostoufi and all the other wonderful people at the Pulitzer Center on Crisis Reporting.

I also wish to thank Edward Kastenmeier, my editor at Anchor, for his constant encouragement to expand on my previous material for this book and to restore many of those details that had ended up on the magazine cutting-room floor. After twenty-two months of labor, it's enormously gratifying to see my work take the permanent form of a book, and I am very grateful to Edward for bringing that to pass. Many thanks also to Sloan Harris and Bill Thomas—my agent and my editor at Doubleday, respectively, but more than that, dear friends—for their forbearance as my "six months" project stretched into nearly two years.

Most of all, I want to express my deepest thanks and gratitude to the six people whose stories make up the heart of this book. All of them spoke to me with remarkable candor, often on some of the most intimate and painful chapters in their lives, and yet they tolerated my incessant questioning with unstinting patience. They did so without any thought of personal reward, only the hope that their stories—and, by extension, those of the many millions of others whose lives have been upended by the turmoils in the Middle East—might be heard.